EVOLUTION

A Fairy Tale
for Grownups

101 questions to shake believers'
blind faith in the theory

RAY
COMFORT

Bridge-Logos
Alachua, Florida 32615

Evolution: A Fairy Tale for Grownups

Published by:
Bridge-Logos
Alachua, Florida 32615, USA
www.bridgelogos.com

Printed in the United States of America

Library of Congress Control Number: 2008923829

ISBN 978-0-88270-585-9

Unless otherwise indicated, Scripture quotations are from the *New King James* version, ©1979, 1980, 1982 by Thomas Nelson Inc., Publishers, Nashville, Tennessee.

Scripture quotations designated NIV are from the *New International Version*, © 1973, 1978, 1984 by the International Bible Society. Published by Zondervan Bible Publishers, Grand Rapids, Michigan.

Cover, page design, and production by Genesis Group (www.genesis-group.net)

"If you make up a story that isn't true, handing it down over a number of centuries doesn't make it any truer!"

—RICHARD DAWKINS

Introduction

nce upon a time there was a man who became disillusioned about God. Instead of believing that God made everything we see, he formed a theory that all this amazing order and complexity came from nothing and randomly evolved over time. As time passed, many people began to believe that this theory was actually true... a scientifically verifiable fact. *Evolution: A Fairy Tale for Grownups* will show you, *from the mouths of experts*, that Darwin's theory is still just that—a theory. It will shake your faith in the theory, because if you believe that Darwinian evolution is scientifically defensible, your faith is completely unfounded.

This book will no doubt be seen by some as "quote mining." This is the practice of taking a quote (often out of its context), and using it in a way that was never intended by the author. However, every gold nugget is legitimately mined out of its context. No one seriously values the earth that encases the gold. So, when I uncover an evolutionary expert quietly admitting that he has no evidence to back up his theory, I don't see any value in the soil of his surrounding words. I merely extract what I believe is of value for those who want to discover the truth about the theory of evolution.

Many who hear about evolution often are not sure what these scientific phrases mean. So, in an effort to broaden our understanding of the issues, here is a very short lesson on the basics. A "transitional form" is a fossil showing one form of life evolving (or changing) to create another, new form of life. Darwinian evolution (as proposed by Charles Darwin) states that mankind and primates (the monkey family) have a common ancestor. To back up the theory, some evolutionists have even created full-color illustrations of hunched apes growing taller over millions of years, then standing upright. To be very simplistic: the universe began with a "big bang" where something suddenly came from nothing, and from there water formed, primitive life appeared in the water, it came up on land, became male and female primates, then eventually evolved into modern man. In other words, simple life forms "transitioned" from one species into another until apes became men and women. However, there is a big problem for those who believe this theory. Scientists can't find any legitimate "missing link" between apes and man in the fossil record. Fossils provide the historical record of plants, animals, and human bones that lie beneath the soil or in the rocks.

After searching and studying quotes from paleontologists, I am convinced that those who spout evolution are guilty of paleontological quackery. Most of them would put Disney "imagineers" out of work. For years I have listened to poker-faced evolutionists' bluffing that they had a "few" transitional forms that could fit "inside a single coffin." But after doing some research, I know that they have nothing in their hand. They are bankrupt. There are no uncontested transitional forms in the fossil record. The following quote from Indiana University's website explains:

According to the theory of evolution, the "descent with modification" road to humans (or any other group, for that matter) is paved with a sequence of transitional fossils... But fortunately, *some* members of some of those groups were fossilized, and *a few of those* are found from time to time, giving us the *hit-or-miss, very spotty record* of fossils which has led us to *hypothesize* [imagine] that picture of a branched tree of being which we call evolution (emphasis added).[1]

The problem is that the transitional forms in the fossil record aren't "few," "hit or miss," or "very spotty." They're simply absent altogether. They don't exist, except in the imaginations of those who represent this pseudo-science called "Evolution."

I've also observed that believers in evolution speak the language of the founder of their faith—something I call "the language of speculation." This dialect is made up of words such as "we believe," "perhaps," "maybe," "possibly," etc. Darwin's *Origin of Species* uses the language of speculation around 800 times.[2] Modern speculations of evolution are nebulous—they are like puffy white clouds. They look impressive until you study them and see that they change with the wind.

---

1. Larry Flammer, "Classroom Cladogram of Vertebrate/Human Evolution" <www.indiana.edu/~ensiweb/lessons/c.bkgrnd.html>.

2. "It has been estimated that no fewer than 800 phrases in the subjunctive mood (such as '*Let us assume,*' or '*We may well suppose,*' etc.) are to be found between the covers of Darwin's alone."—L. Merson Davies, *The Bible and Modern Science* (London: Pickering and Inglis, 1953), p. 7.

In 1982 a Gallup Poll asked Americans if they believed that God created mankind. An amazing 82 percent said that they believed He did. Thirty-five years later, in 2007, the same question was asked, and 81 percent said they thought that God created man.[3] So despite more than fifty years of school children and television viewers being force-fed evolution, belief in the theory increased only 1 percent. It seems that the average American isn't easily fooled.

I don't claim to be a great expert on the subject of evolution, but I have quoted well-known evolutionists who are. They reveal *in their own words* the unscientific nature of that in which they have so blindly placed their faith. So it's now up to you to make a choice about whether you are a believer or not, and then follow the implications. All I ask is that, as you read this book, you keep in mind the wise words of Richard Dawkins: "And, next time somebody tells you that something is true, why not say to them: 'What kind of evidence is there for that?' And if they can't give you a good answer, I hope you'll think very carefully before you believe a word they say."

---

3. "Evolution, Creationism, Intelligent Design" <www.gallup.com/poll/21814/ Evolution-Creationism-Intelligent-Design.aspx>.

QUESTION *1*

In what year did *USA Today* report: "Paleontologists have discovered a new skeleton in the closet of human ancestry that is likely to force science to revise, if not scrap, current theories of human origins"? The discovery left scientists confused, saying, "Lucy may not even be a direct human ancestor after all." (A.) 2001. (B.) 1991. (C.) 1981.

ANSWER: (A.) 2001 (Tim Friend, "Discovery rocks human-origin theories," USA Today, March 21, 2001 <www.usatoday.com/news/science/2001-03-21-skull.htm>).

IN-DEPTH COMMENTS:

"Paleontologists in Africa have found a 3.5-million-year-old skull from what they say is an entirely new branch of the early human family tree, a discovery that threatens to overturn the prevailing view that a single line of descent stretched through the early stages of human ancestry. The discoverers and other scientists of human evolution say they are not necessarily surprised by the findings, but certainly confused. Now it seems that the fossil species *Australopithecus afarensis*, which lived from about four million to three million years ago and is best known from the celebrated Lucy skeleton, was not alone on the African plain. Lucy may not even be a direct human ancestor after all."

—John Noble Wilford, "Skull May Alter Experts' View of Human Descent's Branches," *The New York Times*, March 22, 2001.

"The evidence given above makes it overwhelmingly likely that Lucy was no more than a variety of pygmy chimpanzee, and walked the same way (awkwardly upright on occasions, but mostly quadrupedal). The 'evidence' for the alleged transformation from ape to man is extremely unconvincing."

—Albert W. Mehlert (paleoanthropology researcher), "Lucy: Evolution's Solitary Claim for Ape/Man," *CRS Quarterly*, Vol. 22, No. 3, p. 145.

"Evidence from fossils now points overwhelmingly away from the classical Darwinism which most Americans learned in high school . . . The missing link between man and the apes . . . is merely the most glamorous of a whole hierarchy of phantom creatures. In the fossil record, missing links are the rule . . . The more scientists have searched for the transitional forms between species, the more they have been frustrated."

—Jerry Adler, "Is Man a Subtle Accident?" *Newsweek*, November 3, 1980.

QUESTION *2*

Who said it? "An honest man, armed with all the knowledge available to us now, could only state that, in some sense, the origin of life appears at the moment to be almost a miracle, so many are the conditions which would have had to have been satisfied to get it going." (**A.**) Richard Dawkins. (**B.**) Francis Crick. (**C.**) Carl Sagan.

ANSWER: (**B.**) Francis Crick (*Life Itself, Its Origin and Nature*, 1981, p. 88). Francis Crick (1916–2004) was an English molecular biologist, physicist, and neuroscientist who is most noted for being one of the co-discoverers of the structure of the DNA molecule in 1953. He, James D. Watson, and Maurice Wilkins were jointly awarded the 1962 Nobel Prize for Physiology or Medicine "for their discoveries concerning the molecular structure of nucleic acids and its significance for information transfer in living material."

IN-DEPTH COMMENT:

"Leslie Orgel is one of the leading figures in origin-of-life research since many years, and he is one of several researchers who independently from each other proposed in the 1960s the RNA world as a precursor of the current DNA/protein world. Gerald Joyce is also a top scientist in the field. The authors argue in a joint article published in *The RNA World*, 2nd edition (2000), p. 68, on solid chemical grounds that, because of the complex and stereospecific chemistry required, 'the de novo appearance of oligonucleotides on the primitive earth would have been a near miracle.'.... They go on to say that although the presumed RNA World should be considered a milestone and a plateau in the early history of the earth, the concept 'does not explain how life originated' (p.74). They conclude (p. 74): 'One can sketch out a logical order of events, beginning with prebiotic chemistry and ending with DNA/protein based life. However, it must be said that the details of these events remain obscure and are not likely to be known in the near future.'"

—Albrecht Moritz, "The Origin of Life," October 31, 2006 <www.talkorigins.org/faqs/abioprob/originoflife.html>.

QUESTION 3

Fill in the blank. Well-known evolutionary paleontologist David Kitts said, "Despite the bright promise that pale-ontology provides a means of 'seeing' evolution, it has presented some nasty difficulties for evolutionists the most notorious of which is the presence of 'gaps' in the fossil record. Evolution requires _____ between species and paleontology does not provide them."
(A.) missing links. (B.) much more fossil evidence.
(C.) intermediate forms.

ANSWER: (C.) intermediate forms (*Evolution*, Vol. 28, September 1974, p. 467). Although faced with no paleon-tological way to show one species changing into another, Kitts holds on to his belief in evolution.

IN-DEPTH COMMENTS:

"Given the fact of evolution, one would expect the fossils to document a gradual steady change from ancestral forms to the descendants. But this is not what the pale-ontologist finds. Instead, he or she finds gaps in just about every phyletic series."

—Ernst Mayr (Professor Emeritus, Museum of Comparative Zoology at Harvard University), *What Evolution Is*, 2001, p. 14.

"A persistent problem in evolutionary biology has been the absence of intermediate forms in the fossil record. Long-term gradual transformations of single lineages are rare and generally involve simple size increase or trivial phenotypic effects. Typically, the record consists of successive ancestor-descendant lineages, morphologically invariant through time and unconnected by intermediates."

—P. G. Williamson, *Palaeontological Documentation of Speciation in Cenozoic Molluscs from Turkana Basin*, 1982, p. 163.

"The majority of major groups appear suddenly in the rocks, with virtually no evidence of transition from their ancestors."

—D. Futuyma, *Science on Trial: The Case for Evolution*, 1983, p. 82.

QUESTION *4*

Fill in the blank. Evolutionist Dr. Tim White, an anthropologist at the University of California, Berkeley, said, "The problem with a lot of anthropologists is that they want so much to find a hominid[4] that _____." (A.) they unfortunately stretch the facts. (B.) they jump ahead of themselves. (C.) any scrap of bone becomes a hominid bone.

ANSWER: (C.) any scrap of bone becomes a hominid bone ("Hominoid collarbone exposed as dolphin's rib," *New Scientist*, April 28, 1983, p. 199).

---

4. A hominid is any member of the biological family Hominidae (the "great apes"), and includes modern and extinct humans, chimpanzees, gorillas, and orangutans.

IN-DEPTH COMMENTS:

"Evolutionists present much of their finds as if they were compelling and factual explanations to human evolution. In fact, they base their conclusions on mere speculation and often the flimsiest of 'finds.' Many discoveries of supposed hominids consist of only a mouth fragment, a leg bone, a hip bone, or a knee joint. On this alone, they have considered it to be a hominid. They even name it, reconstruct what it looked like, and present it to the public as a fact. Some of these finds have turned out to be those of a pig, donkey, or the result of a hoax. One hoax consisted of someone placing a human skull with an ape's jaw. Evolutionists declared it to be a hominid for fifty years without having done an in-depth study of it. Some finds consist of an assortment of fragments found miles apart and then placed together to look as though they came from the same individual. Sometimes rocks as simple as those found in any backyard are called tools of hominids and are pictured in books. Footprints that look

identical to any person's today are sometimes declared in books and accepted as those of hominids. The brow ridge that supposedly marked the hominid appears only in one skull."

—Doug LaPointe, "Top Evidences Against the Theory of Evolution" <http://emporium.turnpike.net/C/cs/evid4.htm>.

"A long-enduring and regrettable effect of the success of the *Origin [of Species]* was the addiction of biologists to

unverifiable speculation... This situation, where scientific men rally to the defense of a doctrine they are unable to define scientifically, much less demonstrate with scientific rigour, attempting to maintain its credit with the public by the suppression of criticism and the elimination of difficulties, is abnormal and undesirable in science."
—Evolutionist W. R. Thompson, Introduction to *The Origin of Species* 6th Edition (New York: E. P. Dutton & Co., 1956), p. xxii.

QUESTION 5

Who said it? "To postulate that the development and survival of the fittest is entirely a consequence of chance mutations[5] seems to me a hypothesis based on no evidence and irreconcilable with the facts. These classical evolutionary theories are a gross oversimplification of an immensely complex and intricate mass of facts, and it amazes me that they are swallowed so uncritically and so readily, and for such a long time, by so many scientists without a murmur of protest." (A.) Alexander Fleming. (B.) Gabriel Fahrenheit. (C.) Sir Ernst Chain.

ANSWER: (C.) Sir Ernst Chain, co-holder of 1945 Nobel Prize for developing penicillin (Ronald W. Clark, *The Life of Ernst Chain* [New York: St. Martin's Press, 1985], pp. 147–148).

IN-DEPTH COMMENT:

"'Survival of the fittest' and 'natural selection.' No matter what phraseology one generates, the basic fact remains

---

5. In biology, mutations are changes to the base pair sequence of the genetic material of an organism.

the same: any physical change of any size, shape or form is strictly the result of purposeful alignment of billions of nucleotides (in the DNA). Nature or species do not have the capacity for rearranging them, nor adding them. Consequently no leap (saltation) can occur from one species to another. The only way we know for a DNA to be altered is through a meaningful intervention from an outside source of intelligence: one who knows what it is doing, such as our genetic engineers are now performing in their laboratories."

—I. L. Cohen (Officer of the Archaeological Institute of America, Member New York Academy of Sciences), *Darwin Was Wrong: A Study in Probabilities* (New York: New Research Publications, Inc., 1984), p. 209.

QUESTION *6*

True or False? There is ample fossil evidence to support that mankind evolved from ape-like creatures.

ANSWER: False. "Species that were once thought to have turned into others have been found to overlap in time with these alleged descendants. In fact, the fossil record does not convincingly document a single transition from one species to another." —S. M. Stanley, *The New Evolutionary Timetable: Fossils, Genes, and the Origin of Species* (New York: Basic Books, 1981), p. 95.

IN-DEPTH COMMENTS:

"... the gradual morphological transitions between presumed ancestors and descendants, anticipated by most biologists, are missing."

—David E. Schindel (Curator of Invertebrate Fossils, Peabody Museum of Natural History), "The Gaps in the Fossil Record," *Nature*, Vol. 297, 27 May 1982, p. 282.

"Indeed, it is the chief frustration of the fossil record that we do not have empirical evidence for sustained trends in the evolution of most complex morphological adaptations."

—Stephen J. Gould and Niles Eldredge, "Species Selection: Its Range and Power," *Nature*, Vol. 334, 7 July 1988, p. 19.

QUESTION 7

Which well-known publication reported this? "In extraordinary ways, modern archeology is affirming the historical core of the Old and New Testaments, supporting key portions of crucial biblical stories." (**A.**) *Time.* (**B.**) *Newsweek.* (**C.**) *Reader's Digest.*

ANSWER: (**C.**) *Reader's Digest* (Jeffery L. Sheler, "Is the Bible True?" June 2000).

IN-DEPTH COMMENTS:

Following the 1993 discovery in Israel of a stone containing the inscriptions "House of David" and "King of Israel," *Time* magazine reported, "The writing—dated to the 9th century B.C., only a century after David's reign—described a victory by a neighboring king over the Israelites… The skeptics' claim that David never existed, is now hard to defend."

—Michael D. Lemonick, "Are The Bible's Stories True?" *Time,* June 24, 2001.

"During the past four decades, spectacular discoveries have produced data corroborating the historical backdrop of the Gospels. In 1968, for example, the skeletal remains of a crucified man were found in a burial cave in northern Jerusalem... There was evidence that his wrists may have been pierced with nails. The knees had been doubled up and turned sideways and an iron nail (still lodged in the heel bone of one foot) driven through both heels. The shinbones appeared to have been broken, perhaps corroborating the Gospel of John."

—Jeffery L. Sheler, "Is the Bible True?" *Reader's Digest*, June 2000.

There is nothing in the geological records that runs contrary to the view of conservative creationists, that God created each species separately.

"At the present stage of geological research, we have to admit that there is nothing in the geological records that runs contrary to the view of conservative creationists, that God created each species separately, presumably from the dust of the earth."

—Dr. Edmund J. Ambrose (Emeritus Professor of Cell Biology, University of London), *The Nature and Origin of the Biological World* (John Wiley & Sons, 1982), p. 164.

QUESTION 8

Fill in the blank. Evolutionist Richard Dawkins glibly states, "Feathers are modified reptilian _____," a widely held view among evolutionists. (**A.**) skin folds. (**B.**) scales. (**C.**) fibrous keratin.

ANSWER: (**B.**) scales. However, this is impossible, as Dr. Jonathan Sarfati explains: Because scales are folds in skin, while feathers are complex structures with a barb, barbules, and hooks. Feathers also originate in a totally different way than scales, from follicles inside the skin in a manner akin to hair. Also, feather proteins (f-keratins) are biochemically different from skin and scale proteins (a-keratins). One researcher concluded: "At the morphological level feathers are traditionally considered homologous with reptilian scales. However, in development, morphogenesis, gene structure, protein shape and sequence, and filament formation and structure, feathers are different" (Jonathan Sarfati, "Climbing Mount Improbable: A review of Richard Dawkins' book," 1998 <www.trueorigin.org/dawkrev2.asp>).

IN-DEPTH COMMENT:

"Paleontologists had long been aware of a seeming contradiction between Darwin's postulate of gradualism… and the actual findings of paleontology. Following phyletic lines through time seemed to reveal only minimal gradual changes but no clear evidence for any change of a species into a different genus or for the gradual origin of an evolutionary novelty. Anything truly novel always seemed to appear quite abruptly in the fossil record."

—E. Mayr, *One Long Argument: Charles Darwin and the Genesis of Modern Evolutionary Thought* (Cambridge: Harvard University Press, 1991), p. 138.

QUESTION *9*

Charles Darwin had great concern that in his day there was a lack of evidence regarding the fossil record. He admitted that "we cannot prove that a single species has changed." A century and a half later, does the fossil record prove macroevolution as a scientific fact?

ANSWER: No. In *Darwin's Enigma*, Luther D. Sunderland explains the predicament: "Now, after over 120 years of the most extensive and painstaking geological exploration of every continent and ocean bottom, the picture is infinitely more vivid and complete than it was in 1859. Formations have been discovered containing hundreds of billions of fossils and *our museums now are filled with over 100 million fossils of 250,000 different species.* The availability of this profusion of hard scientific data should permit objective investigators to determine if Darwin were on the right track" (emphasis added [El Cajon, CA: Master Books, 1988], p. 9). The situation hasn't changed any in the last thirty years.

IN-DEPTH COMMENT:

"Given that evolution, according to Darwin, was in a continual state of motion, with ongoing but slow and gradual change accruing over long periods of time, it followed logically that the fossil record should be rife with examples of transitional forms leading from the less to more evolved . . . But when the dust settled, and the fossils were assessed in terms of whether they validated Darwin's evolutionary predictions, a clear picture of slow, gradual evolution, with smooth transitions and transformations from fossils of one period to another, was not forthcoming. Instead of filling the gaps in the fossil record with so-called missing links, most paleontologists found themselves facing a situation in which there were only gaps in the fossil record, with no evidence of transformational intermediates between documented fossil species."

—Jeffrey H. Schwartz, *Sudden Origins: Fossils, Genes, and the Emergence of Species* (New York: John Wiley & Sons, 1999), p. 89.

QUESTION *10*

True or False? The First Law of Thermodynamics states that matter and energy can be neither created nor destroyed.

ANSWER: True. Essentially this means that the conditions that we know hold true in our present universe prevent any possibility of matter springing out of nothing today. To say that no new matter is being created today is to agree with the Bible's statement that "the heavens and the earth were finished" (Genesis 2:1), that God "rested" from His work of creation (2:2).

IN-DEPTH COMMENT:

"First Law of Thermodynamics: Energy can be changed from one form to another, but it cannot be created or destroyed. The total amount of energy and matter in the Universe remains constant, merely changing from one form to another. The First Law of Thermodynamics (Conservation) states that energy is always conserved; it cannot be created or destroyed. In essence, energy can be converted from one form into another."

—Michael J. Farabee, Ph.D., Online Biology Book, 2007 <www.emc. maricopa.edu/faculty/farabee/BIOBK/BioBookEner1.html>.

QUESTION *11*

One famous alleged dino-bird link was *Mononykus*, claimed to be a "flightless bird." The cover of a nationally recognized magazine even illustrated it with feathers, although not the slightest trace of feathers had been found. Later evidence indicated that "*Mononykus* was clearly not a bird... it clearly was a fleet-footed fossorial [digging] theropod."[6] What magazine ended up in this embarrassing situation? (**A.**) *National Geographic.* (**B.**) *Time.* (**C.**) *Science.*

ANSWER: (**B.**) *Time* (Australia, April 26, 1993).

IN-DEPTH COMMENT:

"The researchers found lots of Mononykus bones while digging over the past few years, but one in particular

---

6. D. P. Prothero and R. M. Schoch, eds., *Major Features of Vertebrate Evolution* (Knoxville, TN: University of Tennessee Press, 1994), pp. 160–177.

convinced them they'd found a bird. Mononykus had a keel—a prominent ridge that extends forward from the breastbone—to which the muscles that allow flight would attach. With arms instead of wings, Mononykus obviously couldn't fly. But the keel, says Norell, betrays its bird heritage.

"Not everyone is convinced. 'It's very interesting as whatever it is,' says Storrs Olson, a curator of birds at the Smithsonian Institution, 'but it's not a bird.' He thinks the keeled breastbone looks much more like the sternum of a mole, a digging creature, than the sternum of a bird. And trying to make digging hooks out of a bird's wings, says Olson, would be 'like trying to make a backhoe out of an airplane.' Other researchers speculate that the keel came from another animal altogether and was mistakenly lumped in with the Mononykus bones. A better interpretation of the evidence, they say, would be to call Mononykus a birdlike dinosaur."

—Kathy Svitil, "Bird or mole? Mononykus olecranus, a bird-like fossil with claws instead of wings," *Discover*, January 1994.

QUESTION *12*

Which book in the Bible reveals that the seasons are caused by the changing positions of the earth in relation to the sun, written more than 3,000 years before modern science discovered that fact? (A.) Psalms. (B.) Genesis. (C.) Job.

ANSWER: (B.) Genesis. Genesis 1:14 says, "And God said, Let there be lights in the firmament of the heaven to divide the day from the night; and let them be for signs, and for seasons, and for days, and years."

IN-DEPTH COMMENTS:

"The changing position of the Earth's tilt is the reason for the differences in temperature and length of daylight that distinguish the seasons. When the Northern Hemisphere is leaning toward the sun, the warmth of direct rays causes spring and then summer in that part of the globe. When the Northern Hemisphere is leaning away from the sun, the cooling effects of more indirect sunlight cause autumn and winter. Because the astronomical

position of the Earth causes the seasons, the start of spring, summer, autumn, and winter is marked by special days that correspond to different points in the Earth's orbit."

—National Geographic Xpeditions, "A Reason for the Season" <www.nationalgeographic.com/xpeditions/activities/07/season.html>.

"We account the Scriptures of God to be the most sublime philosophy. I find more sure marks of authenticity in the Bible than in any profane history whatsoever."
—Sir Isaac Newton

"Young men, as you go forth, remember that I, an old man, who has known only science all his life, say unto you that there are no truer facts than the facts found within the Holy Scriptures."

—James Dwight Dana, in an address to Yale seniors. Dana was the foremost American geologist of the nineteenth century, whose *Manual of Geology* was on the shelf of almost every American geologist.

QUESTION *13*

Fill in the blank. Textbook author and biologist Dr. Gary Parker said, "In most people's minds, fossils and evolution go hand in hand. In reality, fossils are a great embarrassment to _____ and offer strong support for the concept of creation." (**A.**) evolutionary theory. (**B.**) biological convergence theory. (**C.**) plate tectonics theory.

ANSWER: (**A.**) evolutionary theory (quoted in Willem Glashouwer and Paul Taylor, *The Origin of Species* video). Dr. Parker began his teaching career as an atheist and evolutionist. En route to his degrees in biology/chemistry, biology/physiology, and an Ed.D. in biology/geology, he realized the arguments for evolution were so weak that he could no longer believe them.

IN-DEPTH COMMENTS:
"If evolution were true, we should find literally millions of fossils that show how one kind of life slowly and gradually changed to another kind of life. But missing links are the trade secret, in a sense, of palaeontology. The point is, the links are still missing. What we really find are gaps that sharpen up the boundaries between kinds.

It's those gaps which provide us with the evidence of creation of separate kinds. As a matter of fact, there are gaps between each of the major kinds of plants and animals. Transition forms are missing by the millions. What we do find are separate and complex kinds, pointing to creation."

—Dr. Gary Parker, quoted in Willem Glashouwer and Paul Taylor, *The Origin of Species* (Mesa, AZ: Eden Films and Standard Media, 1983).

"... Gould and the American Museum people are hard to contradict when they say there are no transitional fossils. As a palaeontologist myself, I am much occupied with

Gould and the American Museum people are hard to contradict when they say there are no transitional fossils.

the philosophical problems of identifying ancestral forms in the fossil record. You say that I should at least 'show a photo of the fossil from which each type of organism was derived.' I will lay it on the line—there is not one such fossil for which one could make a watertight argument. The reason is that statements about ancestry and descent are not applicable in the fossil record. Is Archaeopteryx the ancestor of all birds? Perhaps yes, perhaps no; there is no way of answering the question. It is easy enough to make up stories of how one form gave rise to another, and to find reasons why the stages should be favoured by natural selection. *But such stories are not part of science, for there is no way of putting them to the test"* (emphasis added).

—Dr. Colin Patterson (Senior Palaeontologist, British Museum of Natural History, London), quoted in Luther Sunderland, *Darwin's Enigma* (El Cajon, CA: Master Books, 1988), pp. 88–90.

QUESTION *14*

Who said it? "With few exceptions, radically new kinds of organisms appear for the first time in the fossil record already fully evolved, with most of their characteristic features present." (**A.**) Dr. T. S. Kemp. (**B.**) Henry Gee. (**C.**) Charles Darwin.

ANSWER: (**A.**) Dr. T. S. Kemp, Curator of Zoological Collections at Oxford University (*Fossils and Evolution*, 1999, p. 253).

IN-DEPTH COMMENTS:

British paleontologist Derek V. Ager admits that there is no evidence for gradual evolution, even though he is an evolutionist: "The point emerges that if we examine the fossil record in detail, whether at the level of orders or of species, we find—over and over again—not gradual evolution, but the sudden explosion of one group at the expense of another."

—Derek V. Ager, "The Nature of the Fossil Record," *Proceedings of the British Geological Association*, Vol. 87, 1976, p. 133.

"Niles Eldredge, curator in the department of invertebrates at the American Museum of Natural History and adjunct professor at the City University of New York, is another vigorous supporter of evolution. But he finds himself forced to admit that the fossil record fails to support the traditional evolutionary view. 'No wonder paleontologists shied away from evolution for so long,' he writes. '*It seems never to happen*. Assiduous collecting up cliff faces yields zigzags, minor oscillations, and the very occasional slight accumulation of change-over millions of years, at a rate too slow to really account for all the prodigious change that has occurred in evolutionary history. When we do see the introduction of evolutionary novelty, *it usually shows up with a bang*, and often with no firm evidence that the organisms did not evolve elsewhere! *Evolution cannot forever be going on someplace else.* Yet that's how the fossil record has struck many a forlorn paleontologist looking to learn something about evolution' (*Reinventing Darwin: The Great Debate at the High Table of Evolutionary Theory*, 1995, p. 95, emphasis added).

"After an immense worldwide search by geologists and paleontologists, the 'missing links' Darwin predicted would be found to bolster his theory are still missing."
—"Creation or Evolution: Does It Really Matter What You Believe?" 2008, p. 21 <www.ucg.org/booklets/EV/fossilrecord.htm>.

QUESTION *15*

True or False? A Chinese farmer glued together the head and body of a primitive bird and the tail and hind limbs of a dinosaur, and in 1999 completely fooled the worldwide scientific community into thinking that they had found the "missing link" between carnivorous dinosaurs and modern birds.

ANSWER: True (*National Geographic*, Vol. 196, November 1999, No. 5). Named "Archaeoraptor," this

fossil find constitutes the most recent evolution fraud…
that we know of. Storrs L. Olson of the Smithsonian
Institution said, "*National Geographic* has reached an all-
time low for engaging in sensationalistic, unsubstantiated,
tabloid journalism" (Open letter to Dr. Peter Raven,
Secretary, National Geographic Society, November 1,
1999 <www.trueorigin.org/birdevoletter.asp>).

IN-DEPTH COMMENT:
"The principal part of a famously fabricated dinosaur
fossil is an ancient fish-eating bird, scientists report.

"The Archaeoraptor fossil was introduced in 1999
and hailed as the missing evolutionary link between
carnivorous dinosaurs and modern birds. It was fairly
quickly exposed as bogus, a composite containing the
head and body of a primitive bird and the tail and hind
limbs of a dromaeosaur dinosaur, glued together by a
Chinese farmer.

"Initial CT scans suggested that the fossil might have
been made up of anywhere from two to five specimens of
two or more species. Chinese and American scientists
now report that the fabricated fossil is made up of two
species. The tail and hind limbs were identified in 2000
as belonging to a *Microraptor zhaoianus*, a small, bipedal,
meat-eating dinosaur with some bird-like features.

"Scientists in the November 21 issue of the journal
Nature report that the avian parts of the false dinosaur-
bird fossil are from one specimen, a fish-eating bird
known as *Yanornis martini*."
—Hillary Mayell, National Geographic News, November 20, 2002
<http://news.nationalgeographic.com/news/2002/11/1120_021120_
raptor.html>.

QUESTION *16*

Who said it? "And we find many of them [major inverte-brate groups] already in an advanced state of evolution, the very first time they appear. It is as though they were just planted there, without any evolutionary history. Needless to say, this appearance of sudden planting has delighted creationists." (**A.**) Niles Eldredge. (**B.**) Carl Sagan. (**C.**) Richard Dawkins.

ANSWER: (C.) Richard Dawkins (*The Blind Watchmaker* [New York: W. W. Norton Co., 1987], p. 229). Evolution-ist Dawkins goes on to say in the next paragraph that all evolutionists "despise so-called scientific creationists" and reject divine creation. He proposes that the fossils

must just ap-
pear like that
because of
"imperfections
in the fossil
record."

IN-DEPTH COMMENTS:

"For all of the animal phyla to appear in one single, short burst of diversification is not an obviously predicable outcome of evolution."

—Peter Ward and Donald Brownlee, *Rare Earth* (Springer, 2000), p. 150.

"One of the most difficult problems in evolutionary paleontology has been the almost abrupt appearance of

the major animal groups—classes and phyla—in full-fledged form, in the Cambrian and Ordovician periods."
—A. G. Fisher, *Grolier Multimedia Encyclopedia*, 1998, fossil section.

"Most orders, classes, and phyla appear abruptly, and commonly have already acquired all the characters that distinguish them."
—Francisco J. Ayala and James W. Valentine, *Evolving: The Theory and Processes of Organic Evolution* (Menlo Park, CA: Benjamin/Cummings Publishing Co., 1979), p. 266.

QUESTION *17*

Fill in the blank. At the end of the 19th century, Robert Wiedersheim listed 100 alleged _____ organs. By the time of the Scopes trial, it was up to 180. This list included: tonsils, coccyx (tail bone), thymus, little toe, male nipples, ear nodes, pineal gland, adenoids, appendix, wisdom teeth, parathyroid, ear muscles, body hair, and the nictitating membrane of the eye. Since then, we have discovered important biological functions for every one of these so-called _____ organs. (A.) variational. (B.) vestigial. (C.) venial.

ANSWER: (B.) vestigial (www.allaboutscience.org). A "vestigial" organ was supposedly something non-functioning, left over from a previous evolutionary stage.

IN-DEPTH COMMENT:
"The list of vestigial organs that was made by the German Anatomist R. Wiedersheim in 1895 included . . . the appendix and coccyx. As science progressed, it was discovered

that all of the organs in Wiedersheim's list in fact had very important functions. For instance, it was discovered that the appendix, which was supposed to be a 'vestigial organ,' was in fact a lymphoid organ that fought against infections in the body. This fact was made clear in 1997: 'Other bodily organs and tissues—the thymus, liver, spleen, appendix, bone marrow, and small collections of lymphatic tissue such as the tonsils in the throat and Peyer's patch in the small intestine—are also part of the lymphatic system. They too help the body fight infection.'

"It was also discovered that the tonsils, which were included in the same list of vestigial organs, had a significant role in protecting the throat against infections, particularly until adolescence. It was found that the coccyx at the lower end of the vertebral column supports the bones around the pelvis and is the convergence point of some small muscles and for this reason, it would not be possible to sit comfortably without a coccyx. In the years that followed, it was realized that the thymus triggered the immune system in the human body by activating the T cells, that the pineal gland was in charge of the secretion of some important hormones, that the thyroid gland was effective in providing steady growth in babies and children, and that the pituitary gland controlled the correct functioning of many hormone glands.

"All of these were once considered to be 'vestigial organs.' Finally, the semi-lunar fold in the eye, which was referred to as a vestigial organ by Darwin, has been found in fact to be in charge of cleansing and lubricating the eyeball."

—Harun Yahya, *Evolution Deceit* (London: Ta-Ha Publishers, 1999).

QUESTION *18*

Who said it? "Science without religion is lame, religion without science is blind." (**A.**) Thomas Edison. (**B.**) Albert Einstein. (**C.**) Ben Franklin.

ANSWER: (**B.**) Albert Einstein (Science, Philosophy and Religion: a Symposium, New York, 1941).

IN-DEPTH COMMENT:

While Albert Einstein didn't believe in a personal God, he didn't consider himself to be an atheist or even a pantheist. In reference to God, he said, "I want to know His thoughts." That's not the talk of pantheism. He also said, "We are in the position of a little child entering a huge library filled with books in many different languages. The child knows someone must have written those books. It does not know how. The child dimly suspects a mysterious order in the arrangement of the books but doesn't know what it is. That, it seems to me, is the attitude of even the most intelligent human being toward God. We see a universe marvelously arranged and obeying certain laws, but only dimly understand these laws. Our limited minds cannot grasp the mysterious force that moves the constellations" (Denis Brian, *Einstein: A Life* [New York: John Wiley and Sons, 1996], p. 186).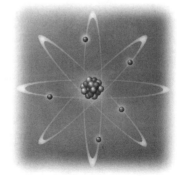

Friedrich Dürrenmatt said of him, "Einstein used to speak

of God so often that I almost looked upon him as a disguised theologian" (Friedrich Dürrenmatt, *Albert Einstein* [Zürich, 1979], p. 12). The great genius once said, "The deeper one penetrates into nature's secrets, the greater becomes one's respect for God" (Brian, *Einstein: A Life*, p. 119). To one of the world's greatest scientists, the order and design in creation give evidence of God.

QUESTION *19*

True or False? Noble Prize winner Sir Ernst Chain once said of the theory of evolution, "I would rather believe in fairy tales than in such wild speculation."

ANSWER: True (Ronald W. Clark, *The Life of Ernst Chain* [New York: St. Martin's Press, 1985], pp. 147–148).

IN-DEPTH COMMENTS:
"The evolution of the genetic machinery is the step for which there are no laboratory models; hence we can speculate endlessly, unfettered by inconvenient facts."
—R. Dickerson, "Chemical Evolution and the Origin of Life," *Scientific American*, September 1978, p. 70.

"A large number of well-trained scientists outside of evolutionary biology and paleontology have unfortunately gotten the idea that the fossil record is far more Darwinian than it is. This probably comes from the oversimplification inevitable in secondary sources: low-level textbooks, semi-popular articles, and so on. Also, there is probably some wishful thinking involved. In the years after Darwin, his advocates hoped to find predictable progressions. In general, *these have not been found*—yet the optimism has died hard, and *some pure fantasy has crept into textbooks.*"

—Paleontologist David Raup, Evolution and the Fossil Record,"
Science, Vol. 213, p. 289 (emphasis added).

QUESTION *20*

Fill in the blank. Renowned evolutionist Stephen Jay Gould wrote, "The absence of fossil evidence for intermediary stages between major transitions in organic design, indeed our inability, even in our imagination, to construct functional intermediates in many cases, has been a persistent and nagging problem for _____

_____." (A.) cataclysmic accounts of evolution.
(B.) fundamental accounts of evolution. (C.) gradualistic accounts of evolution.

ANSWER: (C.) gradualistic accounts of evolution ("Is a new and general theory of evolution emerging?" *Paleobiology,* Vol. 6, No. 1, Winter 1980, p. 127).

IN-DEPTH COMMENTS:

"One hundred and twenty years of paleontological research later, it has become abundantly clear that the fossil record will not confirm this part of Darwin's predictions. Nor is the problem a miserably poor record. The fossil record simply shows that this prediction is wrong."

—N. Eldredge and I. Tattersall, *The Myths of Human Evolution* (New York: Columbia University Press, 1982), pp. 45–46.

"For more than a century biologists have portrayed the evolution of life as a gradual unfolding... Today the fossil record... is forcing us to revise this conventional view."

—S. M. Stanley, *The New Evolutionary Timetable: Fossils, Genes, and the Origin of Species* (New York: Basic Books, 1981), p 3.

QUESTION *21*

Since there are no undisputed transitional forms, German geneticist Richard Goldschmidt, speculated that there must have been quantum leaps from one species to another. He wrote, "The major evolutionary advances must have taken place in single large steps... The many missing links in the paleontological record are sought for in vain because they have never existed: 'the first bird hatched from a reptilian egg.'" His ridiculous theory is called: (A.) cataclysmic escalation. (B.) precipitous equanimity. (C.) punctuated equilibrium.

The many missing links in the paleontological record are sought for in vain because they have never existed.

ANSWER: (C.) punctuated equilibrium (Richard Goldschmidt, *The Material Basis of Evolution*).

IN-DEPTH COMMENTS:

"The old Darwinian view of evolution as a ladder of more and more efficient forms leading up to the present is not borne out by the evidence."

—N. D. Newell, *Why Scientists Believe in Evolution* (American Geological Institute pamphlet, 1984), p 10.

"I believe that our failure to find any clear vector of fitfully accumulating progress . . . represents our greatest dilemma for a study of pattern in life's history."

—S. J. Gould, "The paradox of the first tier: an agenda for paleobiology," *Paleobiology*, Vol. 11, No. 1, Winter 1985, p. 3.

QUESTION *22*

Fill in the blank. In *The Origin of Species* Charles Darwin wrote, "The number of intermediate varieties which have formerly existed on earth must be truly enormous. Why is not every geological formation and every stratum full of such_____? Geology assuredly does not reveal any such finely graduated organic chain; and this is the most obvious and serious objection which can be urged against the theory." (**A.**) fossilized plant matter. (**B.**) intermediate links. (**C.**) invertebrates.

ANSWER: (**B.**) intermediate links. Transitional forms are completely absent from the fossil record. There are no so-called "missing links" that show one animal changing into another. Darwin was worried that the fossil record did not support his theory (Dr. Jonathan Sarfati, *Refuting Evolution*).

IN-DEPTH COMMENTS:
"Many fossils have been collected since 1859, tons of them, yet the impact they have had on our understanding of the relationships between living organisms is barely perceptible . . . In fact, I do not think it unfair to say that fossils, or at least the transitional interpretation of

fossils, have clouded rather than clarified our attempts to reconstruct phylogeny."

—P. L. Forey, "Neontological Analysis Versus Paleontological Stories," *Problems of Phylogenetic Reconstruction* (London: Academic Press, 1982), pp. 120–121.

"Granted an evolutionary origin of the main groups of animals, and not an act of special creation, the absence of any record whatsoever of a single member of any of the phyla in the Pre-Cambrian rocks remains as inexplicable on orthodox grounds as it was to Darwin."

—T. Neville (George Professor of Geology at the University of Glasgow), "Fossils in Evolutionary Perspective," *Science Progress*, Vol. 48, No. 189, January 1960, p. 5.

QUESTION 23

As old as they can make it, the universe still just doesn't offer enough time for life to arise by random chance. One theory says there must be an infinite number of universes existing in parallel dimensions, and we're just lucky enough to live in the one where everything occurred correctly. Adding an infinite number of universes creates an infinite number of chances for things to go right without having to believe in a Creator. This idea is called: (**A.**) The Weak Anthropic Principle. (**B.**) The Strong Anthropic Principle. (**C.**) The Fortunate Anthropic Principle.

ANSWER: (**B.**) The Strong Anthropic Principle (Fred Heeren, *Show Me God*).

IN-DEPTH COMMENTS:

"There is for me powerful evidence that there is something going on behind it all...It seems as though somebody has fine-tuned nature's numbers to make the Universe...The impression of design is overwhelming."
—British astrophysicist Paul Davies, *Superforce: The Search for a Grand Unified Theory of Nature* (New York: Simon & Schuster, 1984), p. 243.

"The laws [of physics]...seem to be the product of exceedingly ingenious design...The universe must have a purpose."
—Paul Davies, *The Cosmic Blueprint: New Discoveries in Nature's Creative Ability to Order the Universe* (New York: Simon & Schuster, 1988), p. 203.

"Don't let the cosmologists try to kid you on this one. They have not got a clue either—despite the fact that they are doing a pretty good job of convincing themselves and others that this is really not a problem. 'In the beginning,' they will say, 'there was nothing—no time, space, matter or energy. Then there was a quantum fluctuation from which...' *Whoa!* Stop right there. You see what I mean? First there is nothing, then there is something. And the cosmologists  try to bridge the two with a quantum flutter, a tremor of uncertainty that sparks it all off. Then they are off and away and before you know it, they have pulled a hundred billion galaxies out of their quantum hats."

—Astronomer Dr. David Darling, "On creating something from nothing," *New Scientist*, Vol. 151, No. 2047, 14 September 1996, p. 49.

QUESTION 24

A group of world famous physicists calculated the odds that all the functional proteins necessary for life might originate by chance. They came up with a figure of one chance in $10^{40,000}$ (that's a 1 with 40,000 zeros after it). Since this is an outrageously small probability, they have adopted the theory that the seeds for life must have come from other planets. This belief is called: (A.) panspermia. (B.) extraterestria. (C.) prespermterestria.

ANSWER: (A.) panspermia ("seeds everywhere"). The fact that any respected scientist would resort to such wild speculation is a good indication of how difficult it is to explain the existence of life without a Creator (Fred Heeren, *Show Me God*).

IN-DEPTH COMMENTS:
Dr. Allan Sandage (winner of the Crawford prize in astronomy), stated: "I find it quite improbable that such order came out of chaos. There has to be some organizing principle. God to me is a mystery but is the explanation for the miracle of existence, why there is something instead of nothing."

—John Noble Wilford, "Sizing Up the Cosmos: An Astronomer's Quest," *New York Times*, March 12, 1991, p. B9.

"Because post-Darwinian biology has been dominated by materialist dogma, the biologists have had to pretend that organisms are a lot simpler than they are. Life itself must be merely chemistry. Assemble the right chemicals, and life emerges. DNA must likewise be a product of chemistry alone. As an exhibit in the New Mexico Museum of Natural History puts it, 'volcanic gases plus lightning equal DNA equals LIFE!' When queried about this fable, the museum spokesman acknowledged that it was simplified but said it was basically true."

—Phillip Johnson, *Weekly Wedge Update*, April 30, 2001, p. 1.

"It is clear that the belief that a molecule of iso-1-cytochrome c or any other protein could appear by chance is based on faith. And so we see that even if we believe that the 'building blocks' are available, they do not spontaneously make proteins, at least not by chance. The origin of life by chance in a primeval soup is impossible in probability in the same way that a perpetual motion machine is impossible in probability... A practical person must conclude that life didn't happen by chance."

—Hubert Yockey, Ph.D., *Information Theory and Molecular Biology* (Cambridge University Press, 1992), p. 257.

QUESTION 25

Since life originating by chance is statistically impossible, astronomer John Barrow and mathematical physicist Frank Tipler were forced to conclude that there must be an intelligence that created life. Unwilling to accept the biblical Creator, they hypothesize that life may evolve to

such an advanced degree that it will become an all-knowing, all-powerful, omnipresent god that then may be able
to create life in the past. They called this concept: (**A.**)
The Weak Anthropic Principle. (**B.**) The Participatory
Anthropic Principle. (**C.**) The Final Anthropic Principle.

ANSWER: (**C.**) The Final Anthropic Principle (John D.
Barrow and Frank J. Tipler, *The Anthropic Cosmological
Principle*, 1986).

IN-DEPTH COMMENTS:
"A common sense interpretation of the facts suggests that
a superintellect has monkeyed with physics, as well as
with chemistry and biology, and that there are no blind forces worth speaking about in nature. The numbers one calculates from the facts seem to me so overwhelming as to put this conclusion almost beyond question."

The more one studies paleontology, the more certain one becomes that evolution is based on faith alone.

—British astrophysicist Fred Hoyle, "The Universe: Past and Present Reflections," *Engineering and Science*, November 1981, p. 12.

"The more one studies paleontology, the more certain
one becomes that evolution is based on faith alone;
exactly the same sort of faith which it is necessary to have
when one encounters the great mysteries of religion."
—Louis T. More, *The Dogma of Evolution* (Princeton, NJ: Princeton
University Press, 1925), p. 160.

QUESTION *26*

In *The Wonderful Egg*, a book written for children, a mother dinosaur lays an egg that hatches into the very first bird. After growing up into a beautiful specimen replete with wings and feathers, it flies up into a tall tree and sings a happy song. (The little bird's song may soon become a funeral dirge when it realizes that it has no one with whom to reproduce.) Since there are no transitional forms, evolutionists have been reduced to this nonsensical idea which they call: (**A.**) cataclysmic escalation. (**B.**) precipitous equanimity. (**C.**) punctuated equilibrium.

ANSWER: (**C.**) punctuated equilibrium (*The FACE That Demonstrates the Farce of Evolution*, Hank Hanegraaff).

IN-DEPTH COMMENTS:

"I agree … that ancestor-descendant relationships cannot be objectively recognized in the fossil record."
—R. M. Schoch, "Evolution Debate," *Science*, April 22, 1983, p. 360.

"The gaps in the record are real, however. The absence of a record of any important branching is quite phenomenal."
—Robert Wesson, *Beyond Natural Selection* (Cambridge, MA: MIT Press, 1991), p. 45.

"No wonder paleontologists shied away from evolution for so long. It never seemed to happen. Assiduous collecting up cliff faces yields zigzags, minor oscillations, and the very occasional slight accumulation of change— over millions of years, at a rate too slow to account for all the prodigious change that has occurred in evolutionary history. When we do see the introduction of evolutionary novelty, it usually shows up with a bang, and often with no firm evidence that the fossils did not evolve elsewhere! Evolution cannot forever be going on somewhere else. Yet that's how the fossil record has struck many a forlorn paleontologist looking to learn something about evolution."

—Niles Eldredge, *Reinventing Darwin: The Great Debate at the High Table of Evolutionary Theory* (New York: Wiley, 1995), p. 95.

QUESTION 27

Who said it? "The remarkable fact is that the values of these numbers seem to have been very finely adjusted to make possible the development of life... Nevertheless, it seems clear that there are relatively few ranges of values for the numbers that would allow the development of any form of intelligent life." (**A.**) Stephen Hawking. (**B.**) Fred Hoyle. (**C.**) Isaac Asimov.

ANSWER: (**A.**) Stephen Hawking (*A Brief History of Time: From the Big Bang to Black Holes* [New York: Bantam Books, 1988], p. 129–130). When he says the values seem to have been finely adjusted to sustain life, he is correct. Such a carefully tuned universe obviously requires an intelligent Creator.

IN-DEPTH COMMENTS:

"Amazing fine tuning occurs in the laws that make this [complexity] possible. Realization of the complexity of what is accomplished makes it very difficult not to use the word 'miraculous' without taking a stand as to the ontological status of the word."

—British astrophysicist George F. Ellis, "The Anthropic Principle: Laws and Environments," *The Anthropic Principle*, F. Bertola and U. Curi, eds. (New York: Cambridge University Press, 1993), p. 30.

"'Somebody had to tune [the universe] very precisely,' concludes Marek Demianski, a Polish cosmologist (quoted in *Science News*, September 3, 1983, p. 152). Stephen Hawking, the Einstein of our time, agrees: 'The odds against a universe like ours coming out of something like the Big Bang are enormous. I think there are clearly religious implications' (John Boslough, *Stephen Hawking's Universe*, p. 121). How the various physical processes are 'fine-tuned to such stunning accuracy is surely one of the great mysteries of cosmology,' remarks P. C. W. Davies, a physicist. 'Had this exceedingly delicate tuning of values been even slightly upset, the subsequent structure of the universe would have been totally different.' 'Extraordinary physical coincidences and apparently accidental cooperation... offer compelling evidence that something is "going on."... A hidden principle seems to be at work' (*The Accidental Universe*, p. 90, p. 110)."

—Holmes Rolston III, "Shaken Atheism: A Look at the Fine-Tuned Universe" <www.religion-online.org/showarticle.asp?title=66>.

"The original 'phase-space volume' [of the universe] requires such... fine tuning that the Creator's aim must have been [precise] to an accuracy of one part in $10^{10^{123}}$. One could not possibly even write the number down in full... [since] it would be a '1' followed by 10^{123} successive '0's—more zeros than the number of elementary particles in the entire universe. Such is the precision needed to set the universe on its course."

—Oxford Physicist Roger Penrose, *The Emperor's New Mind* (New York: Oxford, 1989), p. 344.

QUESTION *28*

Who said it? "Darwin's theory of natural selection has never had any proof, yet it has been universally accepted." (A.) Albert Einstein. (B.) Dr. R. Goldschmidt. (C.) Erik Hollander.

ANSWER: (B.) Dr. R. Goldschmidt, Professor of Zoology, University of California (*Material Basis of Evolution*, 1940).

IN-DEPTH COMMENTS:

"An increasing number of scientists, most particularly a growing number of evolutionists ... argue that Darwinian evolutionary theory is no genuine scientific theory at all ... Many of the critics have the highest intellectual credentials."

—Michael Ruse, "Darwin's Theory: An Exercise in Science," *New Scientist*, June 25, 1981, p. 828.

"There has been no scientific observation of any permanent change in species. There are plenty of proven cases of adaptation, which involves non-genetic changes. There are examples of natural selection changing the balance of populations within a species. Yet there are no known instances of a natural population experiencing a permanent, meaningful change. Observed genetic mutations are, in the natural world, crippling and usually fatal. While there is no doubt about the short-term function of natural selection, its long-term effects are not fully understood. While scientists prefer to point to the examples of birds and moths as proof of the theory of natural selection, they often refuse to see the same examples as contradictory to evolution itself."

—"Theory of Natural Selection," All About Science <www.allaboutscience.org/theory-of-natural-selection-faq.htm>.

QUESTION *29*

True or False? A proposed "missing link" named Java man was based on nothing more than part of a skull, five teeth, and a leg bone.

ANSWER: False. It was only three teeth. Hank Hanegraaff wrote, "All that was found of this claimed originator of humans was a skullcap, three teeth, and a femur. The femur was found 50 feet away from the original skullcap a full year later" (*The FACE That Demonstrates the Farce of Evolution*, 1998, pp. 50–52).

IN-DEPTH COMMENT:

"Late last century a Dutch physician, Eugene Dubois, set sail to the Dutch East Indies (now called Indonesia). Completely enamored by the theory of evolution, he had come to believe for some reason that he would find the elusive 'missing link' between humans and apes in that part of the world.

"In 1892 on the island of Java, he found a thigh-bone, which to all intents and purposes was like that of modern

humans. About a year earlier in the same location he had
found a large skull-cap, and later three teeth. These were
not necessarily from the same individual: the skullcap
and the leg-bone were about 15 meters (50 feet) apart.

"The creature from which the skullcap came
appeared to have had a brain size of 900 cc (about two-
thirds that of the average modern man—one must of
course allow for the difficulty of estimating brain size
from only a part of the skull). There is no reason to insist
that the skullcap and the leg bone came from the same
individual. But Dubois had found his 'missing link' and it
eventually became widely accepted as such, in spite of the
fact that a leading authority had identified two of the
teeth as those of an orangutan, and the other as human.

"'Java man' was trumpeted around the world as indis-
putable proof of human evolution. Textbooks and maga-
zines were filled with fanciful reconstructing of 'Java
man,' who had been given the impressive-sounding scientific name of *Pithecanthropus erectus* ('erect ape-man').

"Naturally, the bones did not show whether their
owner (or owners) had much body hair or not. Yet draw-

ings of 'Java man' all showed the
required amount of hair, the
usual club in the hand, and so on.
Although no face bones had been
found, suitably 'half-ape, half-
man' features were reconstructed
in artists' drawings."

—"Who was Java man?" *Creation*,
Vol. 13, No. 3, June 1991, pp. 22–23
<www.answersingenesis.org/creation/
v13/i3/javaman.asp>.

QUESTION *30*

True or False? "Orce man" (found in the southern Spanish town of Orce in 1982) was hailed as the oldest fossilized human remains ever found in Europe. One year later officials admitted the skull fragment was not human, but probably came from a four-month-old monkey.

ANSWER: False. They admitted that it probably came from a six-month-old donkey ("Skull Fragment May Not be Human," *Knoxville News-Sentinel*, 1983).

IN-DEPTH COMMENT:

"In 1982, a team of three Catalan archaeologists, headed by professor José Gibert, were digging near the village of Orce in Spain. During their dig, they uncovered an unusual bone fragment. A year later, they announced that the fragment belonged to a human child—causing an uproar in the evolutionary community. This discovery placed humans in Europe much earlier than evolutionists had ever predicted. Based on this find, some over-eager scientists reconstructed an entire human. Orce Man, as the find came to be known, was said to represent the oldest human fossil ever discovered in Europe. Later, to the embarrassment of many, the bone was identified as the skull cap of a 6-month-old donkey! No missing link here."

—Brad Harrub, Ph.D. and Bert Thompson, Ph.D., "No Missing Links Here…," May 2002 <www.apologeticspress.org/articles/2509>.

QUESTION *31*

Who said it? "Fossil evidence of human evolutionary history is fragmentary and open to various interpretations. Fossil evidence of chimpanzee evolution is absent altogether." (**A.**) Henry Gee. (**B.**) Julian Huxley. (**C.**) Donald C. Johnson.

ANSWER: (**A.**) Henry Gee ("Palaeontology: Return to the planet of the apes," *Nature*, Vol. 412, 12 July 2001, p. 131).

IN-DEPTH COMMENTS:

"The simple fact is that no proof whatever has been found indicating that one species evolves into another. The fossil record is simply a series of still pictures of species that existed at one time. They do not show how one species evolves into another. Transitional fossils have not been found. The fossil record shows new species appearing suddenly without any ancestors. What scientific investigation indicates is that the species are immutable and that when mutations occur they do not become new species. For example, evolutionists have been experimenting with fruit flies for years in the hope of demonstrating evolution at work. But the fruit flies have stubbornly refused to develop into anything but more fruit

Numerous scientists ... tell us that there is "no doubt" how man originated. If only they had the evidence.

flies, despite all kinds of stimuli, including radiation. Some mutations have occurred, but nothing to suggest the beginnings of a new species.

"Even Dr. Stephen Jay Gould, a passionate defender of evolution, has written, 'The fossil record with its abrupt transitions offers no support for gradual change.' As Darwin wrote in *The Origin of Species*, the geological record is extremely imperfect... and (this fact) will to a large extent explain why we do not find interminable varieties, connecting together all the extinct and existing forms of life by the finest graduated steps.'"

—Dr. Samuel L. Blumenfeld, "Theory of Evolution: Fact or Fairy Tale?" July 10, 2000 <www.worldnetdaily.com/news/article.asp?ARTICLE_ID=16377>.

"The fossil record pertaining to man is still so sparsely known that those who insist on positive declarations can do nothing more than jump from one hazardous surmise to another and hope that the next dramatic discovery does not make them utter fools... As we have seen, there are numerous scientists and popularizers today who have the temerity to tell us that there is 'no doubt' how man originated. If only they had the evidence."

—William R. Fix, *The Bone Peddlers* (New York: Macmillan, 1984), p. 150.

QUESTION 32

True or False? Albert Einstein said, "A little science estranges men from God, but much science leads them back to Him."

ANSWER: False. It was French chemist Louis Pasteur, one of the three main founders of microbiology, to whom we owe the process of *pasteurization*.

IN-DEPTH COMMENTS:

"In science there is no 'knowledge,' in the sense in which Plato and Aristotle understood the word, in the sense which implies finality; in science, we never have sufficient reason for the belief that we have attained the truth... This view means, furthermore, that we have no proofs in science (excepting, of course, pure mathematics and logic). In the empirical sciences, which alone can furnish us with information about the world we live in, proofs do not occur, if we mean by 'proof' an argument which establishes once and for ever the truth of a theory."
—Sir Karl Popper, *The Problem of Induction*, 1953.

"Science, fundamentally, is a game. It is a game with one overriding and defining rule. Rule No. 1: Let us see how far and to what extent we can explain the behavior of the physical and material universe in terms of purely physical and material causes, without invoking the supernatural."
—Richard E. Dickerson (authority on chemical evolution), "The Game of Science," *Perspectives on Science and Faith*, Vol. 44, June 1992, p. 137.

QUESTION *33*

Fill in the blank. Since at least the time of Aristotle (4th century B.C.), people believed that non-living objects could give rise to living organisms. It was common "knowledge" that food left out quickly "swarmed" with

life. With a simple experiment in the mid 1800s, Louis Pasteur disproved the theory of _____.
(**A.**) natural fructifying. (**B.**) simple engenderment. (**C.**) spontaneous generation.

ANSWER: (**C.**) spontaneous generation. Nearly 200 years ago science proved that life cannot originate from lifeless matter. How ironic that evolution is supposedly scientific and yet claims that life originated from lifeless matter.

IN-DEPTH COMMENTS:

"By asking the question, what is spontaneous generation, we are asking: can life generate itself from non-living matter? For centuries, at least back to the 4th century B.C. until the late nineteenth century, people (including scientists) believed that simple living organisms could come into being by 'spontaneous generation.' It was 'common knowledge' that simple organisms like worms, frogs, and salamanders could come from mud, dust, and unpreserved food. Today we know that all apparent spontaneous generation of life has an explanation. We also know that what was thought to be simple life was extremely complicated life. What we have learned is that life comes from life!"

—"What is spontaneous generation?" All About Science <www.allaboutscience.org/what-is-spontaneous-generation-faq.htm>.

"It is a characteristic of the true believer in religion, philosophy and ideology that he must have a set of beliefs, come what may (Hoffer, 1951). Belief in a primeval soup on the grounds that no other paradigm is available is an example of the logical fallacy of the false alternative. In science it is a virtue to acknowledge ignorance. This has been universally the case in the history of science as Kuhn (1970) has discussed in detail. There is no reason that this should be different in the research on the origin of life."

—Hubert P. Yockey, *Information Theory and Molecular Biology* (Cambridge University Press, UK: 1992), p. 336.

QUESTION *34*

True or False? There is plenty of scientific evidence in the fossil record to substantiate that there are transitional forms between species.

ANSWER: False. "The known fossil record is not, and has never has been, in accord with gradualism. What is remarkable is that, through a variety of historical circumstances, even the history of opposition has been obscured. Few modern paleontologists seem to have recognized that in the past century, as the biological historian William Coleman has recently written, 'The majority of paleontologists felt their evidence simply contradicted Darwin's stress on minute, slow, and cumulative changes leading to species transformation.'... Their story has been suppressed."

—S. M. Stanley, *The New Evolutionary Timetable: Fossils, Genes, and the Origin of Species* (New York: Basic Books, Inc., 1981), p. 71.

IN-DEPTH COMMENTS:

"There is another and allied difficulty, which is much more serious. I allude to the manner in which species belonging to several of the main divisions of the animal kingdom suddenly appear in the lowest known fossiliferous rocks."

—Charles Darwin, *The Origin of Species*, p. 348.

"The abrupt manner in which whole groups of species suddenly appear in certain formations, has been urged by several paleontologists—for instance, by Agassiz, Pictet, and Sedgwick—as a fatal objection to the belief in the transmutation of species. If numerous species, belonging to the same genera or families, have really started into life at once, the fact would be fatal to the theory of evolution through natural selection."

—Ibid., p. 344.

The known fossil record is not, and has never has been, in accord with gradualism.

"The most famous such burst, the Cambrian explosion, marks the inception of modern multicellular life. Within just a [supposed] few million years, nearly every major kind of animal anatomy appears in the fossil record for the first time... The Precambrian record is now sufficiently good that the old rationale about undiscovered sequences of smoothly transitional forms will no longer wash."

—Stephen Jay Gould, "An Asteroid to Die For," *Discover*, October 1989, p. 65.

QUESTION 35

Which magazine reported, "We are finding that humans have very, very shallow genetic roots which go back very recently to one ancestor"? (**A.**) *Time*. (**B.**) *Newsweek*. (**C.**) *U.S. News & World Report*.

ANSWER: (**C.**) *U.S. News & World Report* ("The Genetic Eve Gets a Genetic Adam," December 4, 1995).

IN-DEPTH COMMENT:

"Much evidence can be advanced in favor of the theory of evolution—from biology, biogeography and paleontology, but I still think that to the unprejudiced, the fossil record of plants is in favor of special creation. If, however, another explanation could be found for this hierarchy of classification, it would be the knell of the theory of evolution. Can you imagine how an orchid, a duckweed, and a palm have come from the same ancestry, and have we any evidence for this assumption? The evolutionist must be prepared with an answer, but I think that most would break down before an inquisition."

—E. J. H. Corner (Professsor of Botany, Cambridge University, England), "Evolution," in A. M. MacLeod and L. S. Cobley, eds., *Contemporary Botanical Thought* (Chicago: Quadrangle Books, 1961), p. 97.

QUESTION 36

Which famous evolutionist wrote, "It would be very difficult to explain why the universe should have begun in just this way, except as the act of a God who intended to create beings like us"? (**A.**) Sir Alan Carole. (**B.**) Stephen Hawking. (**C.**) Sir Arthur Keith.

ANSWER: (**B.**) Stephen Hawking (*A Brief History of Time: From the Big Bang to Black Holes* [New York: Bantam Books, 1988], p. 127).

IN-DEPTH COMMENTS:

"In the hot big bang model described above, there was not enough time in the early universe for heat to have flowed from one region to another. This means that the initial state of the universe would have to have had exactly the same temperature everywhere in order to account for the fact that the microwave back-ground has the same temperature in every direction we look. The initial rate of expansion also would have had to be chosen very precisely for the rate of expansion still to be so close to the critical rate needed to avoid recollapse. This means that the initial state of the universe must have been very carefully chosen indeed if the hot big bang model was correct right back to the beginning of time. It would be very difficult to explain why the universe should have begun in just this way, except as the act of a God who intended to create beings like us."

—Stephen Hawking, *A Brief History of Time*, p. 127.

NASA astronomer John O'Keefe stated in an interview: "We are, by astronomical standards, a pampered, cosseted, cherished group of creatures . . . If the Universe had not been made with the most exacting precision we could never have come into existence. It is my view that these circumstances indicate the universe was created for man to live in."

—Quoted in Fred Heeren, *Show Me God* (Wheeling, IL, Searchlight Publications, 1995), p. 200.

"Upon receiving the first data about the edges of the universe from the COBE space probe in 1992, project leader George Smoot remarked, 'It's like looking at God.'

"Astronomer Geoffrey Burbidge, an atheist, was so dismayed by the 1992 findings of the COBE spacecraft and confirming experiments, he complained that 'his peers were rushing off to join the 'First Church of the Big Bang.' Other atheists, recognizing the theological implications, started coming to the fore. In early 1993, the Council for Democratic and Secular Humanism ran an article in their magazine *Free Inquiry* entitled, 'Does the Big Bang Prove the Existence of God?' Even the prestigious British journal Nature enlisted its physics editor, John Maddox, to write an editorial entitled 'Down with the Big Bang.' There was no doubt in the minds of all those people about the theistic implications of general relativity and the big bang."

—Ralph O. Muncaster, "A Finely-Tuned Universe: What Are the Odds?" <www.beliefnet.com/story/127/story_12717_1.html>.

"There may be some deep questions about the cosmos that are forever beyond science. The mistake is to think that they are therefore not beyond religion too. I once asked a distinguished astronomer…to explain the Big Bang to me. He did so to the best of his (and my) ability, and I then asked what it was about the fundamental laws of physics that made the spontaneous origin of space and time possible. 'Ah,' he smiled, 'now we move beyond the realm of science. This is where I have to hand over to our good friend, the chaplain.' But why the chaplain? Why not the gardener or the chef? Of course chaplains, unlike chefs and gardeners, *claim* to have some insight into ultimate questions. But what reason have we ever been given for taking their claims seriously? Once again, I suspect that my friend, the professor of astronomy, was using the Einstein/Hawking trick of letting 'God' stand for 'That which we don't understand.'"[7]

—Richard Dawkins, "Snake Oil and Holy Water," *Forbes ASAP*, October 4, 1999.

QUESTION *37*

True or False? *Science* magazine reported in 1984 that shells from living snails were carbon dated as being 7,000 years old.

ANSWER: False. It reported that carbon dating suggested that snails, which were alive, were 27,000 years old (A. C. Riggs, "Major carbon-14 deficiency in modern snail shells from southern Nevada springs," *Science*, Vol. 224, 6 April 1984, pp. 58–61).

---

7. Dawkins is referring to Einstein's quote "God does not play dice with the universe," and Hawking's description of his science as an attempt to "understand the mind of God."

IN-DEPTH COMMENTS:

"Today our duty is to destroy the myth of evolution, considered as a simple, understood, and explained phenomenon which keeps rapidly unfolding before us. The deceit is sometimes unconscious, but not always, since some people, owing to their sectarianism, purposely overlook reality and refuse to acknowledge the inadequacies and falsity of their beliefs."

—Pierre-Paul Grasse (Former President, French Acadamie des Science), *Evolution of Living Organisms* (New York: Academic Press, 1977), p. 8.

"There are no detailed Darwinian accounts for the evolution of any fundamental biochemical or cellular system, only a variety of wishful speculations. It is remarkable that Darwinism is accepted as a satisfactory explanation for such a vast subject—evolution—with so little rigorous examination of how well its basic theses work in illuminating specific instances of biological adaptation or diversity."

—Molecular biologist James Shapiro, "In the Details . . . What?" *National Review*, 19 September 1996, pp. 62–65.

QUESTION 38

True or False? The fossil record gives an abundance of scientific proof for Darwin's theory of evolution.

ANSWER: False. "Scientists concede that their most cherished theories are based on embarrassingly few fossil fragments and that huge gaps exist in the fossil record"

("Puzzling Out Man's Ascent," *Time* magazine, November 7, 1977).

IN-DEPTH COMMENTS:

"Any physical theory is always provisional, in the sense that it is only a hypothesis: you can never prove it…Each time new experiments are observed to agree with the predictions the theory survives, and our confidence in it is increased; but…no matter how many times the results of experiments agree with some theory, you can never be sure that the next time the result will not contradict the theory. On the other hand, you can disprove a theory by finding even a single observation that disagrees with the predictions of the theory."

—Stephen Hawking, *A Brief History of Time: From the Big Bang to Black Holes* (New York: Bantam Books, 1988), p. 10.

"Gaps in the fossil record—particularly those parts of it that are most needed for interpreting the course of evolution—are not surprising."

—G. L. Stebbins, *Darwin to DNA, Molecules to Humanity* (San Francisco: W. H. Freeman & Co., 1982), p. 107.

"The fossil record itself provided no documentation of continuity—of gradual transition from one animal or plant to another of quite different form."

—S. M. Stanley, *The New Evolutionary Timetable: Fossils, Genes and the Origin of Species* (New York: Basic Books, 1981), p. 40.

"The lack of ancestral or intermediate forms between fossil species is not a bizarre peculiarity of early metazoan history. Gaps are general and prevalent throughout the fossil record... Gaps between higher taxonomic levels are general and large."

—R. A. Raff and T. C. Kaufman, *Embryos, Genes, and Evolution: The Developmental-Genetic Basis of Evolutionary Change* (Indiana University Press, 1991), pp. 34–35.

QUESTION *39*

True or False? Albert Einstein was an atheist.

ANSWER: False. He called himself an agnostic. He said, "My position concerning God is that of an agnostic. I am convinced that a vivid consciousness of the primary importance of moral principles for the betterment and ennoblement of life does not need the idea of a law-giver, especially a law-giver who works on the basis of reward and punishment." —*The Expanded Quotable Einstein* (Princeton University Press), pp. 216–217.

IN-DEPTH COMMENT:
"Einstein did, however, retain from his childhood religious phase a profound faith in, and reverence for, the harmony and beauty of what he called the mind of God as it was expressed in the creation of the universe and its laws. Around the time he turned 50, he began to articulate more clearly—in various essays, interviews and letters—his deepening appreciation of his belief in God, although a rather impersonal version of one. One particular evening in 1929, the year he turned 50, captures Einstein's middle-age deistic faith. He and his wife were at a dinner party in Berlin when a guest expressed a belief in astrology. Einstein ridiculed the notion as pure

superstition. Another guest stepped in and similarly disparaged religion. Belief in God, he insisted, was likewise a superstition.

"At this point the host tried to silence him by invoking the fact that even Einstein harbored religious beliefs. 'It isn't possible!' the skeptical guest said, turning to Einstein to ask if he was, in fact, religious. 'Yes, you can call it that,' Einstein replied calmly. 'Try and penetrate with our limited means the secrets of nature and you will find that, behind all the discernible laws and connections, there remains something subtle, intangible and inexplicable. Veneration for this force beyond anything that we can comprehend is my religion. To that extent I am, in fact, religious.'"

—Walter Isaacson, "Einstein & Faith," *Time*, April 05, 2007 <www.time.com/time/magazine/article/0,9171,1607298,00.html>.

QUESTION *40*

Is there any undeniable empirical evidence that human fossils are genetically linked to primates?

ANSWER: No. "Amid the bewildering array of early fossil hominoids, is there one whose morphology marks it as man's hominid ancestor? If the factor of genetic variability is taken into account, the answer appears to be no" (Robert Eckhardt, *Scientific American*, Vol. 226, January 1972, p. 94).

IN-DEPTH COMMENTS:

"Homo erectus has been found throughout the world. He is smaller than the average human of today, with a proportionately smaller head and brain cavity. However, the brain size is within the range of people today and studies of the middle ear have shown that he was just like current Homo sapiens. Remains are found throughout the world in the same proximity to remains of ordinary humans, suggesting coexistence. Australopithecus africanus and Peking man were presented as ape-men missing links for years, but are now both considered Homo erectus."

—"Human Evolution: Frauds & Mistakes," All About Creation <www.allaboutcreation.org/human-evolution.htm>.

"As I have implied, students of fossil primates have not been distinguished for caution when working within the logical constraints of their subject. The record is so astonishing that it is legitimate to ask whether much science is yet to be found in this field at all."

—Lord Solly Zuckerman, M.A., M.D., D.Sc., *Beyond the Ivory Tower* (New York: Taplinger Pub. Co., 1970), p.64.

QUESTION *41*

True or False? Charles Darwin said, "But, as by this theory innumerable transitional forms must have existed, why do we not find them embedded in countless numbers in the crust of the earth?"

ANSWER: True (*The Origin of Species*, chapter 6). Darwin goes on in the next paragraph to say that he believes the transitional forms ("missing links") are missing because the fossil record is "incomplete." Yet here we are almost 150 years later, and all the missing links are still missing. Animals always show up in the fossil record *fully formed*. There are no undisputed transitional forms.

IN-DEPTH COMMENTS:

"Author Luther Sunderland saw the problems with the fossil record, so he determined to get the definitive answer from the top museums themselves. Sunderland interviewed five respected museum officials, recognized authorities in their individual fields of study, including representatives from the American Museum, the Field Museum of Natural History in Chicago, and the British Museum of Natural History. None of the five officials were able to offer a single example of a transitional series of fossilized organisms that document the transformation of one kind of plant or animal into another."

—Randall Niles, "Problems with the Fossil Record," All About the Journey <www.allaboutthejourney.org/problems-with-the-fossil-record.htm>.

"To the question why we do not find rich fossiliferous deposits belonging to these assumed earliest periods prior to the Cambrian system, I can give no satisfactory answer... The case at present must remain inexplicable, and may be truly urged as a valid argument against the views here entertained."

—Charles Darwin, *The Origin of Species*, pp. 350–351.

"The fossil record had caused Darwin more grief than joy. Nothing distressed him more than the Cambrian explosion, the coincident appearance of almost all complex organic designs."

—Stephen J. Gould, *The Panda's Thumb* (New York: W. W. Norton, 1980), pp. 238–239.

QUESTION *42*

True or False? Discovered by Reiner Protsch von Zieten, "Hahnhöfersand Man" (a "missing link" between Neanderthals and modern humans) was later discredited.

ANSWER: True. On February 18, 2005, Protsch was forced to retire in disgrace after a Frankfurt University panel ruled that throughout his career he had "fabricated data and plagiarized the work of his colleagues." They found that he systematically lied about the age of human skulls, dating them tens of thousands of years old, even though they were much younger ("Anthropologist resigns in 'dating disaster,'" February 19, 2005 <www.worldnet-daily.com/news/article.asp?ARTICLE_ID=42940>).

IN-DEPTH COMMENTS:

"The number of years that modern humans are thought to have overlapped with Neanderthals in Europe is shrinking fast, and some scientists now say that figure could drop to zero. Neanderthals lived in Europe and western Asia from 230,000 to 29,000 years ago, petering out soon after the arrival of modern humans from Africa. There is much debate on exactly how Neanderthals went extinct. Theories include climate change and the possession of inferior tools compared to those made by modern humans. Anthropologists also disagree on whether modern humans and Neanderthals are the same species and interbred. Now, some scientists dispute whether they lived side-by-side at all in Europe."

—"Neanderthals and Modern Humans May Have Never Met," May 9, 2006 <www.foxnews.com/story/0,2933,194702,00.html>.

"Despite the excited and optimistic claims that have been made by some paleontologists, no fossil hominid species can be established as our direct ancestor."

—Evolutionist and Harvard professor Richard C. Lewontin, *Human Diversity* (Scientific American Library, 1995), p. 163.

QUESTION *43*

True or False? To illustrate Darwinian evolution's "natural selection," the *Encyclopedia Britannica* used two photos, one showing a light-colored moth and a dark-colored moth against a light background, and then against a dark background. This "peppered moth" evidence of evolution was later proved to be fraudulent.

ANSWER: True (Judith Hooper, *Of Moths and Men: An Evolutionary Tale* (New York: W. W. Norton & Co., 2002), p. 377).

IN-DEPTH COMMENT: "The problems with using the peppered moths as an evolutionary icon only begin there. There also is a serious problem with those images that adorn so many textbooks. The problem is—*the images were faked!*...One paper described how it was done—*dead moths were glued to the tree.* University of Massachusetts biologist Theodore Sargent helped glue moths onto trees for a NOVA documentary. He says textbooks and films have featured 'a lot of fraudulent photographs' (emphasis in original).

"The theory about the moths 'evolving camouflage' for survival was totally false. And, even though many of the writers and textbook publishers know the truth, they are still using the images today.

"Also consider that dark moths and light moths have always been around. There was no new genetic material created to form a black moth. This 'textbook story' is nothing more than gene frequencies shifting back and forth, by natural selection, between populations. But realize, we still are dealing with a single created kind. The moths are still moths! They did not evolve into spiders, cats, or humans. Yet, sadly, the peppered moths nevertheless are being used as 'proof' for evolution. Young people need to understand that while the moth population always had the built-in ability to vary in color, the moths never had the ability to become anything other than moths."

—Brad Harrub, Ph.D., "Peppered with Dishonesty" <www.apologeticspress.org/articles/2365>.

QUESTION 44

Which book of the Bible said that blood is the source of life and health, thousands of years before modern science discovered the fact? (**A.**) Leviticus. (**B.**) Genesis. (**C.**) Hebrews.

ANSWER: (**A.**) Leviticus. Leviticus 17:11 says, "For the life of the flesh is in the blood, and I have given it to you upon the altar to make atonement for your souls; for it is the blood that makes atonement for the soul."

IN-DEPTH COMMENTS:

"Blood carries gases, nutrients and waste products through the body. Blood also fights infections, heals wounds and performs many other vital functions. There is no substitute for blood. It cannot be made or manufactured. Donors are the only source of blood for patients who need it."

—"What Is Blood?" America's Blood Centers <www.americas-blood.org/go.cfm?do=Page.View&pid=11>.

"It was not realized until the discovery of the circulation of the blood by the creationist scientist William Harvey, in about 1620, that biological 'life' really is maintained by the blood, which both brings nourishment to all parts of the body and also carries away its wastes. Its spiritual truth is even more significant. The blood, when shed on the altar, would serve as an 'atonement' (literally, 'covering') for the soul of the guilty sinner making the offering. In fact, the 'life' of the flesh is actually its 'soul,' for 'life' and 'soul' both translate the same Hebrew word (*nephesh*) in this text. When the blood was offered, it was thus an offering of life itself in substitution for the life of the sinner who deserved to die."

—Henry Morris, Ph.D., "Life in the Blood" <www.icr.org/index.php?module=articles&action=view&ID=1823>.

QUESTION *45*

True or False? The famed "Nebraska man" was derived from a single tooth, which was later found to be from an extinct dog.

ANSWER: False. It was later found to be from an extinct pig (John Reader, *Missing Links* [London: William Collins Sons & Co., 1981], p. 110).

IN-DEPTH COMMENT:

"In 1922, Henry Fairfield Osborn, the director of the American Museum of Natural History, declared that he had found a fossil molar tooth belonging to the Pliocene period in western Nebraska near Snake Brook. This tooth allegedly bore common characteristics of both man and ape. An extensive scientific debate began surrounding this fossil, which came to be called 'Nebraska man,' in which some interpreted this tooth as belonging to *Pithecanthropus erectus*, while others claimed it was closer to human beings. Nebraska man was also immediately given a 'scientific name,' *Hesperopithecus haroldcooki*.

"Many authorities gave Osborn their support. Based on this single tooth, reconstructions of Nebraska man's head and body were drawn. Moreover, Nebraska man was even pictured along with his wife and children, as a whole family in a natural setting. All of these scenarios were developed from just one tooth. Evolutionist circles placed such faith in this 'ghost man' that when a researcher named William Bryan opposed these biased conclusions relying on a single tooth, he was harshly criticized.

"In 1927, other parts of the skeleton were also found. According to these newly discovered pieces, the tooth belonged neither to a man nor to an ape. It was realized that it belonged to an extinct species of wild American pig called *Prosthennops.* William Gregory entitled the article published in *Science* in which he announced the truth, '*Hesperopithecus* Apparently Not an Ape Nor a Man.' Then all the drawings of *Hesperopithecus haroldcooki* and his 'family' were hurriedly removed from evolutionary literature."

—Harun Yahya, "The Nebraska Man Scandal" <www.darwinism-refuted.com/origin_of_man_16.html>.

QUESTION *46*

Fill in the blank. Molecular biologist Harry Rubin wrote, "Life, even in bacteria, is _____." (A.) too intricate to ever be fully understood. (B.) too complex to have occurred by chance. (C.) not easily explained by evolution.

ANSWER: (B.) is too complex to have occurred by chance ("Life, Even in Bacteria, Is Too Complex to Have Occurred by Chance" in Henry Margenau and Roy Varghese, eds., *Cosmos, Bios, Theos*, p. 203). Amazingly, Professor Rubin goes on to say he believes life was "created," but that he rejects the "literal interpretation" of what he calls "the Bible story." A few sentences later, he maintains that he still believes in evolution.

IN-DEPTH COMMENT:

"Now imagine 10^{50} blind persons [that's 100,000 billion billion billion billion billion people; standing shoulder to shoulder, they would more than fill our entire planetary system] each with a scrambled Rubik cube and try to conceive of the chance of them all simultaneously arriving at the solved form. You then have the chance of arriving by random shuffling [random variation] of just one of the many biopolymers on which life depends. The notion that not only the biopolymers but the operating program of a living cell could be arrived at by chance in a primordial soup here on Earth is evidently nonsense of a high order."

The theory replaces God with an even more incredible deity— omnipotent chance.

—Sir Fred Hoyle and Chandra Wickramasinghe, *Evolution from Space* (New York: Simon & Schuster, 1984), p. 176.

QUESTION 47

Fill in the blank. H. S. Lipson, Professor of Physics, University of Manchester, UK, wrote, "Evolution became in a sense a _____; almost all scientists have accepted it, and many are prepared to 'bend' their observations to fit in with it." (A.) kind of brainwashing. (B.) scientific religion. (C.) set of blinders.

ANSWER: (**B.**) scientific religion ("A Physicist Looks at Evolution," *Physics Bulletin*, Vol. 31, May 1980, p. 138).

IN-DEPTH COMMENTS:

"For the scientist who has lived by his faith in the power of reason, the story ends like a bad dream. He has scaled the mountains of ignorance; he is about to conquer the highest peak; as he pulls himself over the final rock, he is greeted by a band of theologians who have been sitting there for centuries."

—Robert Jastrow (self-proclaimed agnostic), *God and the Astronomers* (New York: W. W. Norton, 1978), p. 116.

"The irony is devastating. The main purpose of Darwinism was to drive every last trace of an incredible God from biology. But the theory replaces God with an even more incredible deity—omnipotent chance."

—T. Rosazak, *Unfinished Animal* (1975), pp. 101–102.

"Contrary to the popular notion that only creationism relies on the supernatural, evolutionism must as well, since the probabilities of random formation of life are so tiny as to require a 'miracle' for spontaneous generation tantamount to a theological argument."

—Chandra Wickramasinghe (Professor of Applied Math & Astronomy, University College, Cardiff), cited in Norman L. Geisler, *Creator in the Courtroom: Scopes II* (Mieford, MI: Mott Media, 1982), p. 151.

QUESTION 48

In what year did *Science Digest* publish this quote? "The remarkable fact is that all the physical evidence we have for human evolution can still be placed, with room to spare, inside a single coffin.[8] ... Modern apes, for instance, seem  to have sprung out of no-where. They have no yesterday, no fossil record. And the true origin of modern humans—of upright, naked, tool-making, big-brained beings—is, if we were to be honest with ourselves, an equally mysterious matter." **(A.)** 1982. **(B.)** 1972. **(C.)** 1962.

ANSWER: **(A.)** 1982 (Dr. Lyall Watson, "The Water People," *Science Digest*, May 1982, p. 44).

IN-DEPTH COMMENTS:
"The fossil record—in defiance of Darwin's whole idea of gradual change—often makes great leaps from one form to the next. Far from the display of intermediates to be expected from slow advance through natural selection, many species appear without warning, persist in fixed form and disappear, leaving no descendants. Geology assuredly does not reveal any finely graduated organic chain, and this is the most obvious and gravest objection which can be urged against the theory of evolution."
—Steve Jones, *Almost Like a Whale: The Origin of Species Updated* (London: Doubleday, 1999), p. 252.

"All paleontologists know that the fossil record contains precious little in the way of intermediate forms; transi-

---

8. The "coffin" would be empty. There is no empirical evidence in the fossil record for human evolution.

tions between major groups are characteristically abrupt. Gradualists usually extract themselves from this dilemma by invoking the extreme imperfection of the fossil record."
—Stephen J. Gould, *The Panda's Thumb* (New York: W.W. Norton, 1980), p. 189.

"What is missing are the many intermediate forms hypothesized by Darwin, and the continual divergence of major lineages into the morphospace between distinct adaptive types."
—Robert L. Carroll, "Towards a new evolutionary synthesis," *Trends in Evolution and Ecology*, Vol. 15, No. 1, January 2000, p. 27.

QUESTION 49

Fill in the blank. Dr. Michael Walker, Senior Lecturer of Anthropology at Sydney University, said, "One is forced to conclude that many scientists and technologists pay lip-service to Darwinian theory, only because it _____." (A.) supposedly excludes a Creator. (B.) is supposedly the only 'scientific' explanation. (C.) is supposedly the 'educated' explanation.

ANSWER: (A.) supposedly excludes a Creator (*Quadrant*, October 1982, p. 44).

IN-DEPTH COMMENTS:

"All of us who study the origin of life find that the more we look into it, the more we feel that it is too complex to have evolved anywhere. We believe as an article of faith that life evolved from dead matter on this planet. It is just

that its complexity is so great, it is hard for us to imagine that it did."
—Dr. Harold Urey (Nobel Prize winner in Chemistry), *Christian Science Monitor*, 4 January 1962, p. 4.

"The 'standard scientific theory' of evolution is that 'human beings have developed over millions of years from less advanced forms of life, but God had no part in this process' (Shermer, 2002). Dawkins let the cat out of the bag when he observed that 'the *whole point* of the theory of evolution by natural selection was that it provided a *non*-miraculous account of the existence of complex adaptations' (Dawkins, 1986b, p. 249; emphasis added).

"Dawkins had just cited with approval Darwin's response to the geologist Lyell, 'I would give *nothing* for the theory of Natural selection, if it requires miraculous additions at *any one* stage of descent' (Darwin, 1898, 2:6–7) adding with approval, 'For Darwin, any evolution that had to be helped over the jumps by God was *not evolution at all*' (Dawkins, 1986b, p. 249; Dennett, 1995, p. 290). Such 'guided evolution' would be no less 'divine creation' than if it were 'instantaneous'" (Dawkins, 1986, pp. 316–317).
—Stephen E. Jones, "Problems of Evolution" <www.members.iinet. net.au/~sejones/PoE/pe03rlgn.html#rlgnvlnsntgd>.

"In other words, it's Natural Selection or a Creator. There is no middle ground. This is why prominent Darwinists like G. G. Simpson and Stephen Jay Gould, who are not secretive about their hostility to religion, cling so vehemently to natural selection. To do otherwise would be to admit the probability that there is design in nature—and hence a Designer."

—G. S. Johnston, "The Genesis Controversy," *Crisis*, May 1989, p. 17.

QUESTION *50*

Fill in the blank. Professor of paleontology T. N. George stated: "There is no need to apologize any longer for the poverty of the fossil record. In some ways it has become almost unmanageably rich, and discovery is out-pacing integration. The fossil record nevertheless continues to be composed mainly of _____." (**A.**) incomplete skeletons. (**B.**) gaps. (**C.**) newer specimens.

ANSWER: (**B.**) gaps (T. Neville George, "Fossils in Evolutionary Perspective," *Science Progress*, Vol. 48, January 1960, p. 5).

IN-DEPTH COMMENTS:

"It is interesting that all the cases of gradual evolution that we know about from the fossil record seem to involve smooth changes without the appearance of novel structures and functions."

—C. Wills, *Genetic Variability*, 1989, pp. 94–96.

"We seem to have no choice but to invoke the rapid divergence of populations too small to leave legible fossil records."

—S. M. Stanley, *The New Evolutionary Timetable: Fossils, Genes, and the Origin of Species* (New York: Basic Books, 1981), p. 99.

"For over a hundred years paleontologists have recognized the large number of gaps in the fossil record. Creationists make it seem like gaps are a deep, dark secret of paleontology, when just the opposite is the case."
—Joel Cracraft, in Frank Awbrey & William Thwaites, eds., *Evolutionists Confront Creationists* (San Francisco: American Association for the Advancement of Science, 1984).

QUESTION *51*

Who said it? "A long-enduring and regrettable effect of the success of the *Origin [of Species]* was the addiction of biologists to unverifiable speculation... This situation, where scientific men rally to the defense of a doctrine they are unable to define scientifically, much less demonstrate with scientific rigour, attempting to maintain its credit with the public by the suppression of criticism and the elimination of difficulties, is abnormal and undesirable in science." (A.) Creationist Dr. Jonathan Sarfati. (B.) Evolutionist W. R. Thompson. (C.) Evolutionist Stephen J. Gould.

ANSWER: (B.) Evolutionist W. R. Thompson (Introduction to *The Origin of Species* [New York: E. P. Dutton & Co., 1956]).

IN-DEPTH COMMENTS:
"This general tendency to eliminate, by means of unverifiable speculations, the limits of the categories Nature presents to us, is the inheritance of biology from *The Origin of Species*. To establish the continuity required by theory, historical arguments are invoked, even though

historical evidence is lacking. Thus are engendered those fragile towers of hypothesis based on hypothesis, where fact and fiction intermingle in an inextricable confusion."

—W. R. Thompson, "Introduction," to Everyman's Library issue of Charles Darwin's *Origin of Species* (1956 edition).

"I have always been slightly suspicious of the theory of evolution because of its ability to account for any property of living beings (the long neck of the giraffe, for example). I have therefore tried to see whether biological discoveries over the last thirty years or so fit in with Darwin's theory. I do not think that they do. To my mind, the theory does not stand up at all."

—H. S. Lipson, "A Physicist Looks at Evolution," *Physics Bulletin*, Vol. 31, May 1980, p. 138.

"Paleontologists are traditionally famous (or infamous) for reconstructing whole animals from the debris of death. Mostly they cheat... If any event in life's history resembles man's creation myths, it is this sudden diversification of marine life when multicellular organisms took over as the dominant actors in ecology and evolution. Baffling (and embarrassing) to Darwin, this event still dazzles us and stands as a major biological revolution on a par with the invention of self-replication and the origin of the eukaryotic cell. The animal phyla emerged out of the Precambrian mists with most of the attributes of their modern descendants."

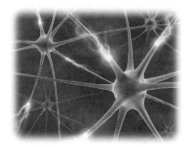

—Stefan Bengtson, "The Solution to a Jigsaw Puzzle," *Nature*, Vol. 345, 28 June 1990, pp. 765–766.

QUESTION 52

Which well-known magazine published an article about carbon dating (the method used to test the age of material) subtitled, "Geologists show that carbon dating can be way off"? (**A.**) *Time*. (**B.**) *National Geographic*. (**C.**) *Newsweek*.

ANSWER: (**A.**) *Time* ("Mistaken by Millenniums," June 11, 1990).

IN-DEPTH COMMENT:

"Carbon dating in many cases seriously embarrasses evolutionists by giving ages that are much younger than those expected from their model of early history. A specimen older than 50,000 years should have too little ^{14}C to measure.

"Laboratories that measure ^{14}C would like a source of organic material with zero ^{14}C to use as a blank to check that their lab procedures do not add ^{14}C. Coal is an obvious candidate because the youngest coal is supposed to be millions of years old, and most of it is supposed to be tens or hundreds of millions of years old. Such old coal should be devoid of ^{14}C. It isn't. *No source of coal has been found that completely lacks ^{14}C.*

"Fossil wood found in 'Upper Permian' rock that is supposedly 250 Ma old still contained ^{14}C (A. A. Snelling, 'Stumping Old-age Dogma,' *Creation*, 1998, 20(4):48–50). Recently, a sample of wood found in rock classified as 'middle Triassic,' supposedly some 230 million years old, gave a ^{14}C date of 33,720 years, plus or minus 430 years (A. A. Snelling, 'Dating Dilemma,' *Creation*, 1999, 21(3):39–41). The accompanying checks showed that the ^{14}C date was not due to contamination and that the 'date' was valid, within the standard (long ages) understanding of this dating system.

"It is an unsolved mystery to evolutionists as to why coal has ^{14}C in it (D. C. Lowe, 'Problems Associated with the Use of Coal as a Source of ^{14}C Free Background Material,' *Radiocarbon*, 1989, 31:117–120), or wood supposedly millions of years old still has ^{14}C present, but it makes perfect sense in a creationist world view."

—"How accurate are Carbon-14 and other radioactive dating methods?" <www.christiananswers.net/q-aig/aig-c007.html>.

QUESTION *53*

True or False? The human "tailbone" is an evolutionary leftover and proof that man once had a tail.

ANSWER: False. The "tailbone" has nothing to do with a tail. It is the base of the spine, and is called the coccyx vertebrae. Among other things, it serves as a shock absorber when the person sits down.

IN-DEPTH COMMENT:

"The 'human tail' is just one example of what evolutionists call a 'vestigial organ.' As the name suggests, these organs are supposed to represent useless remnants of what were once functional and useful organs in our primitive ancestors. As recently as 1971, the *Encyclopedia Britannica* claimed that there were more than 100 vestigial organs in man. Even critically important organs such as the thymus and parathyroid glands were once considered to be vestigial simply because their functions were not understood. As biomedical science has progressed, there are fewer and fewer claims of functionless organs. Despite their diminishing numbers, vestigial organs are still mentioned in textbooks as one of the strongest evidences for evolution and against intelligent design by a Creator. The most frequently cited examples of vestigial organs in man are the coccyx and the appendix.

"The human coccyx, or 'tail bone,' is a group of four or five small vertebrae fused into one bone at the lower end of our vertebral column. Most of us never really think about our 'tail bone' until we fall on it. Evolutionists are dead certain that the coccyx is a vestige of a tail left over from our monkey-like ancestors. The coccyx does occupy the same relative position at the end of our vertebral column as does the tail in tailed primates, but then, where else would it be? The vertebral column is a linear row of bones that supports the head at its beginning and it must end somewhere. Wherever it ends, evolutionists will be sure to call it a vestigial tail.

"Most modern biology textbooks give the erroneous impression that the human coccyx has no real function other than to remind us of the 'inescapable fact' of evolution. In fact, the coccyx has some very important functions. Several muscles converge from the ring-like arrangement of the pelvic (hip) bones to anchor on the coccyx, forming a bowl-shaped muscular floor of the pelvis called the pelvic diaphragm. The incurved coccyx with its attached pelvic diaphragm keeps the many organs in our abdominal cavity from literally falling through between our legs. Some of the pelvic diaphragm

muscles are also important in controlling the elimination of waste from our body through the rectum."
—David N. Menton, Ph.D., "The Human Tail, and Other Tales of Evolution" <www.gennet.org/facts/metro07.html>.

QUESTION 54

True or False? Evolutionists try to claim that the fossils *Protarchaeopteryx robusta* and *Caudipteryx zoui* are "the immediate ancestors of the first birds."

ANSWER: True. However, these two fossils of flightless birds (similar to ostriches) have bird-like teeth and lack the long tail seen in the theropod dinosaurs they are sup-

posedly descended from. Additionally, avian evolution researcher A. Feduccia said, "It is biochemically impossible to evolve flight from such large bipeds with foreshortened forelimbs and heavy, balancing tails," exactly the wrong anatomy for flight (*Science*, Vol. 274, 1996, pp. 720–721).

IN-DEPTH COMMENT:
"Evolutionary ornithologists Larry Martin and Allan Feduccia, strong critics of the dino-to-bird dogma, believe that the fossils are more likely to be flightless birds similar to ostriches. *Caudipteryx* even used gizzard

stones like modern plant-eating birds, but unlike
theropods."
—Ji Qiang, P. J. Currie, et al., "Two feathered dinosaurs from north-
eastern China," *Nature*, Vol. 393, 25 June 1998, pp. 753–761.

QUESTION 55

Which book of the Bible spoke of the earth's free float in
space, thousands of years before modern science discovered the fact? (**A.**) Genesis. (**B.**) Job. (**C.**) Isaiah.

ANSWER: (**B.**) Job. Job 26:7 says, "He stretches out the
north over empty space; He hangs the earth on nothing."
This was written in the Scriptures at a time when scientists believed that the earth sat on the back of a gigantic
animal. Such incredible statements in the Bible (and
there are many) made no sense until we understood that
space has no gravity, and the Earth does indeed hang on
nothing. The skeptic may write this off as being some
sort of stroke of luck on the part of the Bible in getting it
right, but there are so many similar scientific verses that
a reasonable person is left with the thought that they are
absolute proof that the Bible must be supernatural in
origin.

IN-DEPTH COMMENT:
"The Bible talked about the 'circle of the earth' long
before Galileo did, when men thought the earth was flat.
And before man understood astronomy, the Bible said
that God had fixed the stars in the sky, keeping them in
their place. Today we would say that it's gravity that does
that, but again, God beat us to the punch. God is the one

who put the forces in place, who gave order to the universe. And we, by His timing, have come to observe that order and understand the forces. It was this assumption (a God-ordered universe) that was the scientific starting point for many great scientists (Sir Isaac Newton, for example).

"The forces and the order are observable, but what has brought them about? Today scientists are looking for a grand unified field theory—glue that brings quantum theory and astrophysics under one force/theory. Consider that God Himself is the unified field they're looking for. It is God Himself who decides that things will work differently on an astronomical level than on a microscopic level. Size is relative and irrelevant. Things should work the same on both the astronomic and the microscopic levels, but they don't. Hence there are baffled scientists trying to make sense of things, because God is not their starting point. Even if a force is discovered that explains things (like gravity), you're still left with the question of how the force got there."

—"Doesn't modern science invalidate the Bible?" <www.every-student.com/forum/science.html>.

QUESTION *56*

Which two books of the Bible said that the ocean floor contains deep valleys and mountains, thousands of years before modern science discovered the fact? (**A.**) Genesis and Job. (**B.**) Genesis and Isaiah. (**C.**) 2 Samuel and Jonah.

ANSWER: (**C.**) 2 Samuel and Jonah. Second Samuel 22:16 says, "Then the channels of the sea were seen, the foundations of the world were uncovered, at the rebuke

of the LORD, at the blast of the breath of His nostrils."
Jonah 2:6 says, "I went down to the moorings of the
mountains; the earth with its bars closed behind me forever; yet You have brought up my life from the pit, O
LORD, my God."

IN-DEPTH COMMENT:
"Have you ever wondered how the ocean would look
without all that water? How it would look if it were just
dry land? Well, if you're standing on the shore watching
the sandy beach disappear beneath the waves, you may
think that it is probably like a big sandy desert. It's not.
The ocean floor is as varied and irregular as the land we
can see. It has mountains and plains and valleys and
ridges and volcanoes and just about any other land fea-
ture you could name."
—Science & Technology Focus, Office of Naval Research
<www.onr.navy.mil/focus/ocean/regions/oceanfloor1.htm>.

QUESTION 57

Who said it? "If it could be demonstrated that any complex organ existed, which could not possibly have been
formed by numerous, successive, slight modifications,
my theory would absolutely break down." (A.) Charles
Shultz. (B.) Charles Spurgeon. (C.) Charles Darwin.

ANSWER: (C.) Charles Darwin (*The Origin of Species*).
Darwin says in the next sentence, "But I can find out no
such case." If he could have seen the simple sea slug eating
a sea anemone, for example, he would have known that
millions of years would make no difference. If the sea

slug's protective mechanisms were not complete and perfectly operating in its first attack, it would have died (Geoff Chapman, "Sea slugs leave Darwin's theory slipping," *Creation*, Vol. 15, Issue 1, December 1992, pp. 24–25).

IN-DEPTH COMMENTS:

In a keynote address, Dr. Colin Patterson, Senior Paleontologist at the British Museum of Natural History, London, stated: "One of the reasons I started taking this anti-evolutionary view, or let's call it a non-evolutionary view, was last year I had a sudden realization for over twenty years I had thought I was working on evolution in some way. One morning I woke up and something had happened in the night and it struck me that I had been working on this stuff for twenty years and there was not one thing I knew about it. That's quite a shock to learn that one can be so misled so long. Either there was something wrong with me or there was something wrong with evolutionary theory... For the last few weeks I've tried putting a simple question to various people and groups of people.

"Question is: Can you tell me anything you know about evolution, any one thing, that is true? I tried that question on the geology staff at the Field Museum of Natural History and the only answer I got was silence. I tried it on the members of the Evolutionary Morphology Seminar in the University of Chicago, a very prestigious body of evolutionists, and all I got there was silence for a long time and eventually one person said, 'I do know one thing—it ought not to be taught in high school.'"

—Dr. Colin Patterson, address at the American Museum of Natural History, New York City, November 5, 1981.

"It is now approximately half a century since the neo-Darwinian synthesis was formulated. A great deal of research has been carried on within the paradigm it defines. Yet the successes of the theory are limited to the interpretation of the minutiae of evolution, such as the adaptive change in coloration of moths; while it has remarkably little to say on the questions which interest us most, such as how there came to be moths in the first place."

—M. W. Ho and P. T. Saunders, "Beyond neo-Darwinism: An Epigenetic Approach to Evolution," *Journal of Theoretical Biology*, Vol. 78, 1979, p. 589.

QUESTION *58*

Which two books of the Bible spoke of the hydrologic cycle, thousands of years before it was discovered by modern science? (**A.**) Genesis and Acts. (**B.**) Job and Leviticus. (**C.**) Ecclesiastes and Amos.

ANSWER: (C.) Ecclesiastes and Amos. Ecclesiastes says, "All the rivers run into the sea, yet the sea is not full; to the place from which the rivers come, there they return again" (1:7) and "If the clouds are full of rain, they empty themselves upon the earth" (11:3). Amos 9:6 says, "He who builds His layers in the sky, and has founded His strata in the earth; who calls for the waters of the sea, and pours them out on the face of the earth—the Lord is His name."

IN-DEPTH COMMENT:

"Water moves around the world, changes forms, is taken in by plants and animals, but never really disappears. It 'travels' in a large, continuous cycle. We call this the Hydrologic Cycle ('hydro' means water). Together, these five processes—condensation, precipitation, infiltration, runoff, and evapotranspiration—make up the Hydrologic Cycle. Water vapor condenses to form clouds, which result in precipitation when the conditions are suitable. Precipitation falls to the surface and infiltrates the soil or flows to the ocean as runoff. Surface water (e.g., lakes, streams, oceans, etc.), evaporates, returning moisture to the atmosphere, while plants return water to the atmosphere by transpiration."

—NASA's Observatorium, "Hydrologic Cycle" <http://observe.arc. nasa.gov/nasa/earth/hydrocycle/hydro1.html>.

QUESTION 59

Who said it? "Scientists who go about teaching that evolution is a fact of life are great con-men, and the story they are telling may be the greatest hoax ever. In explaining evolution, we do not have one iota of fact." (**A.**) Dr. Nelson Glueck. (**B.**) Colin Powell. (**C.**) Dr. T. N. Tahmisian.

ANSWER: (**C.**) Dr. T. N. Tahmisian of the Atomic Energy Commission (*The Fresno Bee*, August 20, 1959, p. 1-B).

IN-DEPTH COMMENT:

"Considering its historic significance and the social and moral transformation it caused in western thought, one might have hoped that Darwinian theory...a theory of such cardinal importance, a theory that literally changed the world, would have been something more than metaphysics, something more than a myth."

—Molecular biologist Michael Denton, *Evolution: A Theory in Crisis* (Bethesda, MD: Adler & Adler, 1986), p. 358.

QUESTION 60

True or False? *The Journal of Science* reported that scientists may have been a million years off in their belief as to when life appeared on earth.

ANSWER: False. They actually reported that they may have been a *billion* years off (NBC News, August 1999).

IN-DEPTH COMMENTS:

"It is unknown when life first appeared on Earth, which is approximately 4.5 billion years old. The residue of ancient life that the scientists believe they have found existed prior to the end of the 'late heavy bombardment' of the Moon by large objects, a period which ended approximately 3.8 billion years ago, Harrison noted. 'Life is tenacious, and it completely permeates the surface layer of the planet,' Mojzsis said. 'We find life beneath the deepest ocean, on the highest mountain, in the driest desert and the coldest glacier, and deep down in the crustal rocks and sediments.' An unanswered question is

how life originally could have arisen from lifeless molecules and evolved into the already sophisticated isotope fractioning life forms recorded in the Akilia rocks."
—"Scientists Strengthen Case for Life on Earth More Than 3.8 Billion Years Ago," *Science Daily*, July 21, 2006 <www.sciencedaily.com/releases/2006/07/060721090947.htm>.

"We are faced more with a great leap of faith—that gradual progressive adaptive change underlies the general pattern of evolutionary change we see in the rocks—than any hard evidence."
—N. Eldredge and I. Tattersall, *The Myths of Human Evolution* (New York, Columbia University Press, 1982), p. 57.

QUESTION 61

True or False? Human embryos have gill slits, which shows that we have evolved from fish.

ANSWER: False. There are markings on a human embryo which superficially look like they might be "gill slits." But these "pharyngeal clefts" never have any breathing function, and they are
never "slits" or openings. They develop into the thymus gland, parathyroid glands, and middle ear canals—none of which has anything to do with breathing, under water or above water (Don Batten, ed., *The Answers Book* [Green Forest, AR: Master Books, 2000], p. 119).

IN-DEPTH COMMENT:

"Almost from the beginning, evolutionists have attempted to equate the process of evolution with the progressive development of the embryo. During the famous Scopes *'Monkey Trial'* in 1925, for example, lawyers and expert witnesses defending teaching Darwinism in public schools, repeatedly confused evolution with embryology. The lawyers even insisted that evolution must be taught if physicians are to understand the development of babies in the womb! The very word 'evolution' (which means 'unfolding'), was taken from the name of an early theory of embryonic development which proposed that humans are completely preformed in miniature in the fertilized egg, simply 'unfolding' during the development of the baby.

The blind-chance process of Darwinian "evolution" has nothing whatever to do with the exquisitely-controlled process of embryological development.

"Obviously, the blind-chance process of Darwinian 'evolution' has nothing whatever to do with the exquisitely-controlled process of embryological development. Still, evolutionists have long attempted to relate embryology to evolution, presumably in an effort to extrapolate the readily-observable process of embryonic development into the unobservable process of macroevolution. Embryology continues to play a role in current evolutionary dogma. Generations of students have been told, for example, that the human embryo developing in the womb passes through stages of its evolutionary ancestry—even at one point having gills like a fish!"

—David N. Menton, Ph.D., "Is the Human Embryo Essentially a Fish with Gills?" 1997 <www.gennet.org/facts/metro06.html>.

QUESTION *62*

What encyclopedia spoke of evolution as being "impossible"? (A.) Encyclopedia Britannica. (B.) The Creationist's Encyclopedia. (C.) Encyclopedie Francaise.

ANSWER: (C.) Encyclopedie Francaise: "The theories of evolution, with which our studious youth have been deceived, constitute actually a dogma that all the world continues to teach; but each, in his specialty, the zoologist or the botanist, ascertains that none of the explanations furnished is adequate... It results from this summary, that the theory of evolution is impossible."

—P. Lemoine (Director of the Natural History Museum in Paris), "Introduction: De L' Evolution?" *Encyclopedie Francaise*, Vol. 5, 1937, p. 6.

IN-DEPTH COMMENTS:

"Finally, there is only one attitude which is possible as I have just shown: It consists in affirming that intelligence comes before life. Many people will say this is not science, it is philosophy. The only thing I am interested in is fact, and this conclusion comes out of an analysis and observation of the facts."

—G. Salet, *Hasard et Certitude: Le Transformisme devant la Biologie Actuelle* (1973), p. 331.

"It is futile to pretend to the public that we understand how an amoeba evolved into a man, when we cannot tell our students how a human egg produces a skin cell or a brain cell!"

—Dr. Jerome J. Lejeune, Discoverer of the cause of Down's syndrome, Institute de Progenese (Paris), former Professor of Fundamental Cytogenetics.

"Nobody I know in my profession believes it [genetic code] evolved. It was engineered by genius beyond genius, and such information could not have been written any other way...Creation design is like an elephant in the living room. It moves around, takes up an enormous amount of space, loudly trumpets, bumps into us, knocks things over, eats a ton of hay, and smells like an elephant. And yet we have to swear it isn't there!"

—A molecular biologist (speaking on condition of anonymity) who identifies genetic controls for diseases, interviewed by George Caylor, *The Ledger* (Lynchburg, VA), February 17, 2000.

QUESTION 63

Who said it? "I think that if it had been a religion that first maintained the notion that all the matter in the entire universe had once been contained in an area smaller than the point of a pin, scientists probably would have laughed at the idea." (**A.**) Stuart G. Scott. (**B.**) Marilyn vos Savant. (**C.**) Danny M. Goodall.

ANSWER: (**B.**) Marilyn vos Savant (listed in Guinness Book of World Records for highest IQ, at 230), when asked to comment on the 'big bang' theory (*Parade,* February 4, 1996, p. 7).

IN-DEPTH COMMENT:

"The big bang today relies on a growing number of hypothetical entities, things that we have never observed— inflation, dark matter and dark energy are the most prominent examples. Without them, there would be a fatal contradiction between the observations made by astronomers and the predictions of the big bang theory. In no other field of physics would this continual recourse to new hypothetical objects be accepted as a way of bridging the gap between theory and observation. It would, at the least, raise serious questions about the validity of the underlying theory. But the big bang theory can't survive without these fudge factors."

—"Open Letter to the Scientific Community," signed by 405 secular astronomers, scientists, engineers, and researchers, *New Scientist,* May 22, 2004 <www.cosmologystatement.org>.

QUESTION *64*

Which respected scientists, in a joint statement, said it's obvious that it is "almost inevitable that our own measure of intelligence must reflect in a valid way the higher intelligence"? (**A.**) C. David Allis and Carl-Henry Alström. (**B.**) Sir Fred Hoyle and Chandra Wickramasinghe. (**C.**) Sidney Altman and Cecil A. Alport.

ANSWER: (B.) Sir Fred Hoyle and Chandra Wickrama-singhe. "Once we see, however, that the probability of life originating at random is so utterly minuscule as to make it absurd, it becomes sensible to think that the favorable properties of physics on which life depends are in every respect deliberate... It is therefore almost inevitable that our own measure of intelligence must reflect in a valid way the higher intelligence... even to the extreme idealized limit of God... Such a theory is so obvious that one wonders why it is not widely accepted as being self-evident. The reasons are psychological rather than scientific."

—Sir Fredrick Hoyle and Chandra Wickramasinghe, *Evolution from Space* (London: J. M. Dent & Sons, 1981), pp. 130–144.

IN-DEPTH COMMENT:

"Astronomy leads us to a unique event, a universe that was created out of nothing and delicately balanced to provide exactly the conditions required to support life. In the absence of an absurdly improbable accident, the observations of modern science seem to suggest an underlying, one might say, supernatural plan."

—Arno Penzias (Physicist and Nobel laureate), quoted by D. L. Brock in *Our Universe: Accident or Design* (Wits, S. Africa: Star Watch, 1992), p. 42.

QUESTION 65

Which magazine reported this? "The vast majority of artist's conceptions are based more on imagination than on evidence... Artists must create something between an ape and a human being; the older the specimen is said to be, the more ape-like they make it." (**A.**) *Time.* (**B.**) *Science Digest.* (**C.**) *Reader's Digest.*

ANSWER: (**B.**) *Science Digest* (B. Rensberger, "Ancestors: A Family Album," April 1981, p. 41).

IN-DEPTH COMMENTS:

"Echoing the criticism made of his father's *Homo habilis* skulls, he added that Lucy's skull was so incomplete that most of it was 'imagination, made of plaster of Paris,' thus making it impossible to draw any firm conclusion about what species she belonged to."

—Interview with Richard Leakey (Director of National Museums of Kenya, son of Louis Leakey) in *The Weekend Australian*, May 7–8, 1983, Magazine section, p. 3.

"I believe that one day the Darwinian myth will be ranked the greatest deceit in the history of science. When this happens, many people will pose the question: 'How did this ever happen?'"

—Dr. Soren Lovtrup, *Darwinism: The Refutation of a Myth* (Beckingham, Kent: Croom Helm, 1987), p. 422.

QUESTION 66

True or False? In 2004, legendary British philosopher and proponent of atheism Professor Antony Flew renounced his atheism because "the argument to intelligent design is enormously stronger than it was when I first met it."

ANSWER: True. He said, "It now seems to me that the findings of more than fifty years of DNA research have provided materials for a new and enormously powerful argument to design." He admitted he "had to go where the evidence leads."

—Quoted by Rich Deem, "One Flew Over the Cuckoo's Nest?" <www.godandscience.org/apologetics/flew.html>.

IN-DEPTH COMMENTS:

"The DNA Double Helix is one of the greatest scientific discoveries of all time. First described by James Watson and Francis Crick in 1953, DNA is the famous molecule of genetics that establishes each organism's physical characteristics. It wasn't until mid-2001 that the Human

 Genome Project and Celera Genomics jointly presented the true nature and complexity of the digital code inherent in DNA. We now understand that each human DNA molecule is comprised of chemical bases arranged in approximately 3 billion precise sequences. Even the DNA molecule for the single-celled bacterium, *E. coli*, contains enough information to fill all the books in any of the world's largest libraries."

—"DNA Double Helix: Information Code," All About Science <www.allaboutscience.org/dNA-double-helix.htm>.

"Many investigators now consider nucleic acids to be much more plausible candidates for the first self-replicating molecules. The work of Watson and Crick and others has shown that proteins are formed according to the instructions coded in DNA. But there is a hitch. DNA cannot do its work, including forming more DNA, without the help of catalytic proteins, or enzymes. In short, proteins cannot form without DNA, but neither can DNA form without proteins. To those pondering the origin of life, it is a classic chicken-and-egg problem: Which came first, proteins or DNA?"

—John Horgan, Science writer, "In the Beginning . . . ," *Scientific American*, Vol. 264, No. 2, February 1991, p. 103.

QUESTION 67

Which national magazine reported this statement about evolution? "So heated is the debate that one Darwinian says there are times when he thinks about going into a field with more intellectual honesty: the used-car business." (A.) *Time*. (B.) *Science Today*. (C.) *Newsweek*.

ANSWER: (C.) *Newsweek* (Evolutionist Sharon Begley, "Science Contra Darwin," April 8, 1985, p. 80).

IN-DEPTH COMMENT:

"When I began my career as a cosmologist some twenty years ago, I was a convinced atheist. I never in my wildest dreams imagined that one day I would be writing a book purporting to show that the central claims of Judeo-Christian theology are in fact true, that these claims are straightforward deductions of the laws of physics as we now understand them. I have been forced into these conclusions by the inexorable logic of my own special branch of physics."

—Frank Tipler (Professor of Mathematical Physics), *The Physics of Immortality* (New York: Doubleday, 1994), Preface.

QUESTION 68

Who said it? "I find it as difficult to understand a scientist who does not acknowledge the presence of a superior rationality behind the existence of the universe as it is to comprehend a theologian who would deny the advances of science." (**A.**) Wernher von Braun. (**B.**) Nicholas Copernicus. (**C.**) Marie Curie.

ANSWER: (**A.**) Wernher von Braun, the world's most famous rocket scientist, and former head of NASA's Marshall Space Flight Center ("My Faith," *American Weekly*, February 10, 1963).

IN-DEPTH COMMENTS:

"What gambler would be crazy enough to play roulette with random evolution? The probability of dust carried by the wind reproducing Durer's 'Melancholia' is less infinitesimal than the probability of copy errors in the DNA molecule leading to the formation of the eye; besides, these errors had no relationship whatsoever with the function that the eye would have to perform or was starting to perform. There is no law against daydreaming, but science must not indulge in it."

—Pierre-Paul Grasse (French zoologist), *Evolution of Living Organisms* (New York: Academic Press, 1977), p. 104.

"If living matter is not, then, caused by the interplay of atoms, natural forces and radiation, how has it come into being? There is another theory, now quite out of favor, which is based upon the ideas of Lamarck: that if an organism needs an improvement it will develop it, and transmit it to its progeny. I think, however, that we must go further than this and admit that the only acceptable explanation is creation. I know this is an anathema to physicists, as indeed it is to me, but we must not reject a theory that we do not like if the experimental evidence supports it."

—Dr. H. S. Lipson, F.R.S. (Professor of Physics, University of Manchester, UK), "A Physicist Looks at Evolution," *Physics Bulletin*, Vol. 31, May 1980, p. 138.

QUESTION *69*

Who said this regarding the Bible? "Let men of science and learning expound their knowledge and prize and probe with their researches every detail of the records which have been preserved to us from those dim ages. All they will do is to fortify the grand simplicity and essential accuracy of the recorded truths which have lighted so far the pilgrimage of man." (A.) Winston Churchill. (B.) Zola Levitt. (C.) Napoleon.

ANSWER: (A.) Winston Churchill (*Thoughts and Adventures* [Freeport, NY: Books for Libraries Press, 1972], pp. 293–294.

IN-DEPTH COMMENTS:

"We must not build on the sands of an uncertain and ever-changing science . . . but upon the rock of inspired Scriptures."

—Sir Ambrose Flemming, British electrical engineer and inventor.

"I believe that the Bible is to be understood and received in the plain and obvious meaning of its passages; for I cannot persuade myself that a book intended for the instruction and conversion of the whole world should cover its true meaning in any such mystery and doubt that none but critics and philosophers can discover it ... Education is useless without the Bible."

—Daniel Webster, American politician and noted orator.

QUESTION 70

Who said it? "The march of science, falsely so called, through the world may be traced by exploded fallacies and abandoned theories. Former explorers once adored are now ridiculed; the continual wreckings of false hypotheses is a matter of universal notoriety. You may tell where the supposed learned have encamped by the debris left behind of suppositions and theories as plentiful as broken bottles." (**A.**) Charles Spurgeon. (**B.**) Aldous Huxley. (**C.**) Chuck Missler.

ANSWER: (**A.**) Charles Spurgeon (*The Sword and the Trowel*, 1877, p. 197).

IN-DEPTH COMMENTS:
"We have all heard of *The Origin of Species*, although few of us have had time to read it ... A casual perusal of the

classic made me understand the rage of Paul Feyerabend
... I agree with him that Darwinism contains 'wicked
lies'; it is not a 'natural law' formulated on the basis of
factual evidence, but a dogma, reflecting the dominating
social philosophy of the last century."

—Kenneth J. Hsu, "Sedimentary Petrology and Biologic Evolution,"
Journal of Sedimentary Petrology, Vol. 56, September 1986, p. 730.

"As I said, we shall all be embarrassed, in the fullness of
time, by the naiveté of our present evolutionary arguments. But some will be vastly more embarrassed than
others."

—Massimo Piattelli-Palmarini, Principal Research Associate of the
Center for Cognitive Science at MIT, *Inevitable Illusions: How
Mistakes of Reason Rule Our Minds* (New York: John Wiley & Sons,
1994), p. 195.

QUESTION *71*

Fill in the blank. Malcolm Muggeridge, British philosopher, wrote, "I myself am convinced that the theory of
evolution, especially the extent to which it has been
applied, will be one of the _____."
(A.) most important steps toward self-actualization ever
taken in history. (B.) biggest mistakes history has ever
recorded. (C.) the great jokes in the history books of the
future.

ANSWER: (C.) the great jokes in the history books of the
future (Pascal Lectures, University of Waterloo Research,
The Advocate, March 8, 1984, p. 17).

IN-DEPTH COMMENT:

"When it comes to the Origin of Life there are only two possibilities: creation or spontaneous generation. There is no third way. Spontaneous generation was disproved one hundred years ago, but that leads us to only one other conclusion, that of supernatural creation. We cannot accept that on philosophical grounds; therefore, we choose to believe the impossible: that life arose spontaneously by chance!"

—Prominent evolutionist George Wald (Harvard University biochemist and Nobel Laureate), "The Origin of Life," *Scientific American*, May 1954.

QUESTION 72

True or False? The Second Law of Thermodynamics says that the amount of usable energy in the universe is becoming less and less.

ANSWER: True. Essentially this means that things will eventually "wear out." The universe is not eternal; it had a beginning, and will eventually wear out. Twenty-five hundred years before the birth of modern science, when the brightest thinkers were confident that the universe was eternal, the Bible said that the universe would "wear out": "... the heavens are the work of Your hands. *They will perish*, but You remain; *they will all wear out* like a garment" (Psalm 102:25,26, NIV).

IN-DEPTH COMMENT:

"The Second Law of Thermodynamics states that 'in all energy exchanges, if no energy enters or leaves the system, the potential energy of the state will always be less than that of the initial state.' This is also commonly referred to as entropy. A watchspring-driven watch will run until the potential energy in the spring is converted, and not again until energy is reapplied to the spring to rewind it. A car that has run out of gas will not run again until you walk 10 miles to a gas station and refuel the car. Once the potential energy locked in carbohydrates is converted into kinetic energy (energy in use or motion), the organism will get no more until energy is input again. In the process of energy transfer, some energy will dissipate as heat. Entropy is a measure of disorder: cells are *not* disordered and so have low entropy. The flow of energy maintains order and life. Entropy wins when organisms cease to take in energy and die."

—Michael J. Farabee, Ph.D., Online Biology Book, 2007 <www.emc. maricopa.edu/faculty/farabee/BIOBK/BioBookEner1.html>.

QUESTION 73

True or False? The biblical description of creation and the Darwinian theory of evolution are compatible.

ANSWER: False. The Bible says that man was made in the image of God, that every animal brought forth "according to their kinds" (Genesis 1:21) and that "men have one kind of flesh, animals have another, birds another and fish another" (1 Corinthians 15:39).

IN-DEPTH COMMENTS:

"A variation on the theme of evolution is theistic evolution. It states that God initiated life on earth and allowed

evolutionary principles to bring man to where he is—
maybe with a little help from God here and there. At least
this theory includes God. But this theory was developed
in part by Bible believing people who thought that evolution had some merit. In addition, it is an attempt to
answer the many problems existing not only in the fossil
record but also with how life could somehow randomly
form out of nothing. Because of problems like this, some
believe they can be explained by simply adding God to
the picture: God directed evolution.

"For those who hold to the
Bible as the word of God, theistic
evolution should not be a viable
option. The Bible says, '*Know that
the* LORD *is God. It is he who made
us…*' (Psalm 100:3). The Scriptures state that God created…He
said, 'Let there be' and it was so. It
does not say, 'Let there be a slow
development through an evolutionary process.'

" …The land animals were
made differently than man. The
animals were made from the
ground but man was made directly
by God: '*the* LORD *God formed the
man from the dust of the ground
and breathed into his nostrils the
breath of life, and the man became a living being*' (Gen.
2:7). Evolution states that man evolved from life forms
that developed in the ocean. Here, God made man from
the dust of the ground—not the water of the ocean.

"If evolution is true and the Bible is true then how is the formation of Eve explained? She was created out of one of Adam's ribs (Gen. 2:22). There is no way to explain this if theistic evolution is true; that is, unless you want to say that Eve wasn't made from Adam's side. Then, if you do that, you are doubting the very word of God.

"Also, Jesus said in Mark 10:6, '*But at the beginning of creation God "made them male and female."*' The beginning was not evolutionary slime; in the beginning of creation there was Adam and Eve.

"Though this information is brief and far from complete, it should be obvious that theistic evolution and the Scriptures cannot be harmonized."

—Matthew Slick, "Theistic Evolution" <www.carm.org/evolution/evtheistic.htm>.

"The creation account in Genesis and the theory of evolution could not be reconciled. One must be right and the other wrong. The story of the fossils agreed with the account of Genesis. In the oldest rocks we did not find a series of fossils covering the gradual changes from the most primitive creatures to developed forms; but rather, in the oldest rocks, developed species suddenly appeared. Between every species there was a complete absence of intermediate fossils."

—D. B. Gower (biochemist), "Scientists Rejects Evolution," *Kentish Times*, England, December 11, 1975, p. 4.

QUESTION 74

True or False? If people and dinosaurs were created at the same time, the word "dinosaur" would appear in the Bible.

ANSWER: False. The King James Bible was translated in 1611, and it wasn't until 1841 that the word "dinosaur" (from Greek words meaning "terrible lizard") was invented. Is there another word for "dinosaur"? The Hebrew word translated "dragon" in the KJV Bible appears in the Old Testament some 30 times (e.g., Jer. 51:34; Mal. 1:3). In many contexts these could refer to what we now call dinosaurs. Even *Strong's Concordance* lists "dinosaur" as one of the meanings of that Hebrew word (Don Batten, ed., *The Answers Book* [Green Forest, AR: Master Books, 2000], p. 243).

IN-DEPTH COMMENT:

"There is a growing body of evidence that dinosaurs and humans were contemporary. In 1970 newspapers reported the discovery of cave paintings in Zimbabwe. The paintings were made by bushmen who ruled that area from about 1500 B.C., until a couple of hundred years ago. Along with accurate representations of the elephant and the giraffe, is a painting of an Apatosaurus (brontosaurus). These art works have greatly puzzled scientists since bushmen are known to have painted from real life! (*Bible-Science Newsletter* 1970, 2).

"About seventy years ago, Dr. Samuel Hubbard, curator of archaeology in the Oakland (California) Museum, discovered dinosaur carvings on the cliff walls of the Hava Supai Canyon in Arizona. One remarkable carving resembles a Tyrannosaurus. Nearby, dinosaur tracks were preserved in the rock surface. (For a picture of this carving, see our book, *The Mythology of Modern Geology* 1990, 31.)

"When the discovery of what appeared to be human footprints, along with dinosaur tracks (in the Paluxy River bed near Glen Rose, Texas), was reported in the May 1939 issue of *Natural History*, it created a furor that has not subsided to this very day. For decades it seemed obvious to careful observers that this was clear evidence of human/dinosaur co-habitation."

—Wayne Jackson, "Dinosaurs and the Bible," August 5, 1999 <www.christiancourier.com/articles/read/dinosaurs_and_the_bible>.

QUESTION 75

True or False? *Ramapithecus*, once widely regarded as an ancestor of humans, has now been recognized as merely an extinct type of orangutan.

ANSWER: True. "*Ramapithecus:* an extinct group of primates that lived from about 12 to 14 million years ago, for a time regarded as a possible ancestor of Australopithecus and, therefore, of modern humans" (*The Columbia Encyclopedia*).

IN-DEPTH COMMENT:

"Although it was generally an apelike creature, *Ramapithecus* was considered a possible human ancestor on the basis of the reconstructed jaw and dental characteristics of fragmentary fossils. A complete jaw discovered in 1976 was clearly nonhominid, however, and *Ramapithecus* is

now regarded by many as a member of *Sivapithecus*, a
genus considered to be an ancestor of the orangutan."
—*The Columbia Encyclopedia*, Sixth Edition, 2007
<www.bartleby.com/65/e-/E-Ramapith.html>.

QUESTION 76

Who said it? "To suppose that the eye, with all its inim-
itable contrivances for adjusting the focus to different
distances, for admitting different amounts of light, and
for the correction of spherical and chromatic aberration,
could have formed by natural selection, seems, I freely
confess, absurd in the highest degree possible." (**A.**) Albert
Einstein. (**B.**) Charles Darwin. (**C.**) Stephen Hawking.

ANSWER: (**B.**) Charles Darwin (*On the Origin of Species*
[London: J. M. Dent & Sons Ltd., 1971], p. 167). Darwin,
later on in his book, explained how he believed it evolved
anyway and that the "absurdity" was just an illusion.

IN-DEPTH COMMENTS:

"The human eye is enormously complicated—a perfect
and interrelated system of about 40 individual subsystems, including the retina, pupil, iris, cornea, lens and
optic nerve. For instance, the retina has approximately
137 million special cells that respond to light and send
messages to the brain. About 130 million of these cells
look like rods and handle the black and white vision. The
other seven million are cone shaped and allow us to see
in color. The retina cells receive light impressions, which
are translated to electric pulses and sent to the brain via
the optic nerve.

"A special section of the brain called the visual cortex interprets the pulses to color, contrast, depth, etc., which allows us to see 'pictures' of our world. Incredibly, the eye, optic nerve and visual cortex are totally separate and distinct subsystems. Yet, together, they capture, deliver and interpret up to 1.5 million pulse messages a millisecond! It would take dozens of Cray supercomputers programmed perfectly and operating together flawlessly to even get close to performing this task."

—Lawrence O. Richards, *It Couldn't Just Happen* (Nashville: Thomas Nelson, Inc., 1989), pp. 139–140.

"The exquisite order displayed by our scientific understanding of the physical world calls for the divine."

—Vera Kistiakowsky, MIT physicist, quoted in Henry Margenau and Roy Varghese, eds., *Cosmos, Bios, Theos* (La Salle, IL: Open Court, 1992), p. 52.

QUESTION 77

Who said it? "This most beautiful system of the sun, planets, and comets could only proceed from the counsel and dominion of an intelligent and powerful Being." (A.) Stephen Hawking. (B.) Albert Einstein. (C.) Sir Isaac Newton.

ANSWER: (C.) Sir Isaac Newton ("the father of science"), *The Mathematical Principles of Natural Philosophy*, Book III, Andrew Motte, trans. (London: H. D. Symonds, 1803), pp. 310–314 <www.thenagain.info/Classes/Sources/Newton.html>.

IN-DEPTH COMMENTS:

"Professor H. E. Huntley in *The Divine Proportion—A Study In Mathematical Beauty*, poses the evolutionary puzzle of our aesthetic sense thus: 'we might begin by asking whether the universal human thirst for beauty serves a useful purpose. Physical hunger and thirst ensure our bodily survival. The sex drive takes care of the survival of the race. Fear has survival value. But—to put the question crudely—what is beauty for? What personal or evolutionary end is met by the appreciation of a rainbow, a flower or a symphony? At first sight, none.'

Big bang cosmology has become a bandwagon of thought that reflects faith as much as objective truth.

"Huntley suggests that: 'a part of the answer is that [beauty] serves as a lure to induce the mind to embark on creative activity. Beauty is a bait. [However] This view seems to require the existence of 'absolute' beauty, to demand that specimens of beauty antedate the human perception of them, although beauty in its subjective sense is called into existence only at the moment of its appreciation.' And this conclusion is fodder for the objective ontological aesthetic design argument. Of course, if our appreciation of beauty does have an evolutionary (efficient) explanation, this does not exclude the possibility that our appreciation is also the result of (teleological) intelligent design."

—Peter S. Williams, "Intelligent Design, Aesthetics and Design Arguments" <www.arn.org/docs/williams/pw_idaestheticsand-designarguments.htm>.

"Big bang cosmology is probably as widely believed as has been any theory of the universe in the history of Western civilization. It rests, however, on many untested, and in some cases untestable, assumptions. Indeed, big bang cosmology has become a bandwagon of thought that reflects faith as much as objective truth."
—Geoffrey Burbidge, "Why Only One Big Bang?" *Scientific American*, Vol. 266, February 1992, p. 120.

QUESTION 78

True or False? Darwin stated, "Why, if species have descended from other species by insensibly fine gradations, do we not everywhere see innumerable transitional forms? Why is not all nature in confusion instead of the species being, as we see them, well defined?"

ANSWER: True (*On the Origin of Species* (London: John Murray, 1872), pp. 133–134).

IN-DEPTH COMMENTS:

"We do not have any available fossil group which can categorically be claimed to be the ancestor of any other group. We do not have in the fossil record any specific point of divergence of one life form for another, and generally each of the major life groups has retained its fundamental structural and physiological characteristics throughout its life history and has been conservative in habitat."
—G. S. Carter (Professor, Fellow of Corpus Christi College, Cambridge, England), *Structure and Habit in Vertebrate Evolution* (Seattle: University of Washington Press, 1967).

"Paleontologists had long been aware of a seeming contradiction between Darwin's postulate of gradualism . . .
and the actual findings of paleontology. Following phyletic lines through time seemed to reveal only minimal
gradual changes but no clear evidence for any change of
a species into a different genus or for the gradual origin
of an evolutionary novelty. Anything truly novel always
seemed to appear quite abruptly in the fossil record."

—E. Mayr, *One Long Argument: Charles Darwin and the Genesis of
Modern Evolutionary Thought* (Cambridge: Harvard University
Press, 1991), p. 138.

QUESTION 79

Which famous newspaper reported: "Piltdown Man
Hoax Is Exposed"? (**A.**) *The L.A. Times.* (**B.**) *The Dallas
Morning News.* (**C.**) *The New York Times.*

ANSWER: (**C.**) *The New York Times* (November 21, 1953).
The article stated, "Part of the skull of the Piltdown man,
one of the most famous fossil skulls in the world, has
been declared a hoax by authorities at the British Natural
History Museum" <www.pbs.org/wgbh/aso/databank/
entries/do53pi.html>.

IN-DEPTH COMMENT:
"Piltdown Man (Eoanthropus Dawsoni) was once
thought to be a 'missing link' between man and ape. The
first Piltdown fragments were discovered in 1912. There-
after, over 500 scientific essays were written on the
Piltdown Man in a 40-year period. The discovery was
proven to be a deliberate hoax in 1953.

"Piltdown Man consisted of two human skulls, an orangutan jaw, an elephant molar, a hippopotamus tooth, and a canine tooth from a chimpanzee. Sir Kenneth Oakley has determined the human skulls to be approximately 620 years old. They may have belonged to Ona Indians from Patagonia, as the skulls were unusually thick. Thick skulls are a common trait among Ona Indians. The orangutan jaw is around 500 years old, perhaps from Sarawak. The elephant molar is thought to be from Tunisia. The hippopotamus tooth is thought to have come from Malta or perhaps Sicily. The canine tooth belonged to a Pleistocene Chimpanzee.

"The Piltdown remains were purposefully scattered around a quarry in Piltdown, England, so that they could be 'discovered' later as evidence for evolution and the development of man from ape. The skulls had been treated with acid. All of the fossil remains were stained with an iron sulfate solution. The canine tooth was painted brown and patched with bubble gum. The molars were filed down. The portion of the orangutan jaw that connected the jaw to its skull was carefully broken so as not to show evidence that this jaw did not belong to a human skull."

—"Piltdown Man: Test All Data," All About Creation
<www.allaboutcreation.org/piltdown-man.htm>.

QUESTION *80*

Before it was discovered to be a hoax, what age did experts estimate "Piltdown Man" to be? (A.) 500,000 to one million years old. (B.) Four million years old. (C.) Fifty million years old.

ANSWER: (A.) 500,000 to one million years old. According to PBS, "At that time, the skullcap was still believed to be about 500,000 years old. In 1959, however, the recently discovered carbon-14 dating technique was used to show that it was between 520 and 720 years old, the jawbone slightly younger!" ("Piltdown Man is revealed as fake" <www.pbs.org/wgbh/aso/databank/entries/do53pi.html>).

IN-DEPTH COMMENT:

"When the blood of a seal, freshly killed at McMurdo Sound in the Antarctic was tested by carbon-14, it showed the seal had died 1,300 years ago."

—W. Dort Jr., Ph.D. (Geology Professor, University of Kansas), *Antarctic Journal of the United States*, 1971.

QUESTION *81*

What was the name of the amateur geologist who discovered what was thought to be "the evolutionary find of the century" in a gravel pit near the town of Piltdown, England? (A.) Charles Darwin. (B.) Charles Dawson. (C.) Charles Prince.

ANSWER: (**B.**) Charles Dawson (NOVA, "The Boldest Hoax" <www.pbs.org/wgbh/nova/hoax>).

IN-DEPTH COMMENT:

"For decades, a fossil skull discovered in Piltdown, England, was hailed as the missing link between apes and humans. Entire careers were built on its authenticity. Then in 1953, the awful truth came out: 'Piltdown Man' was a fake! ...

"It all started in the early 1900s, when a laborer digging near the village of Piltdown in southern England reportedly found a strange piece of skull that he passed on to Charles Dawson, a local amateur archeologist ...

"'Piltdown Man was a really big deal in 1912, because it was a time when very little was known of human fossil remains,' says historian Richard Milner. 'It was perceived to be the missing link, the fossil that connected humans with apes.' Notably, Piltdown Man was even more spectacular than the celebrated human fossils already discovered on the European continent, such as Neanderthal Man in Germany.

"More remains turned up in Piltdown through 1915, the year before Dawson's death. These included a second partial skull and a strange bone artifact resembling a cricket bat—a fishy find that looked suspiciously like a hoax but was accepted by Woodward as an ancient implement. Forty years later, new scientific tests showed

that Piltdown Man was a forgery, concocted in part from what was probably an orangutan's jaw. Suspicion immediately fell on Dawson, but there were other candidates."
—NOVA, "The Boldest Hoax" <www.pbs.org/wgbh/nova/hoax>.

QUESTION *82*

Which well-known expert in human evolution admitted, "If you brought in a smart scientist from another discipline and showed him the meager evidence we've got he'd surely say, 'Forget it: there isn't enough to go on'"? (**A.**) David Pilbeam. (**B.**) Aldous Huxley. (**C.**) Richard Leakey.

The fossil record is somewhat incomplete as far as the hominids are concerned, and it is all but blank for the apes.

ANSWER: (**A.**) David Pilbeam (quoted in Richard E. Leakey, *The Making of Mankind* [London: Michael Joseph Limited, 1981], p. 43).

IN-DEPTH COMMENT: "Biologists would dearly like to know how modern apes, modern humans and the various ancestral hominids have evolved from a common ancestor. Unfortunately, the fossil record is somewhat incomplete as far as the hominids are concerned, and it is all but blank for the apes. The best we can hope for is that more fossils will be found over the next few years which will fill the present gaps in the evidence.'"
—Richard E. Leakey, *The Making of Mankind* (London: Michael Joseph Limited, 1981), p. 43.

QUESTION *83*

Who said that with no objective truth to stand on, when it comes to man's fossil history, "to the faithful anything is possible"? (**A.**) Albert Einstein. (**B.**) Lord Solly Zuckerman. (**C.**) Winston Churchill.

ANSWER: (**B.**) Lord Solly Zuckerman. "We then move right off the register of objective truth into those fields of presumed biological science, like extrasensory perception or the interpretation of man's fossil history, where to the faithful anything is possible—and where the ardent believer is sometimes able to believe several contradictory things at the same time."

—Lord Solly Zuckerman, Professor of Anatomy at Birmingham University in England, *Beyond the Ivory Tower* (New York: Toplinger Publications, 1970), p. 19.

IN-DEPTH COMMENTS:

"If you thought that science was certain—well, that is just an error on your part."

—Richard Feynman, *The Character of Physical Law* (Cambridge, MA: MIT Press, 1967), p. 77.

"A religious creed differs from a scientific theory in claiming to embody eternal and absolutely certain truth, whereas science is always tentative, expecting that modification in its present theories will sooner or later be found necessary, and aware that its method is one which is logically incapable of arriving at a complete and final demonstration."

—Bertrand Russell, *Religion and Science* (New York: Oxford University Press, 1953).

QUESTION 84

Fill in the blank. "If pressed about man's ancestry, I would have to unequivocally say that all we have is _____." (A.) definitive proof. (B.) a series of transitional forms. (C.) a huge question mark.

ANSWER: (C.) a huge question mark (Richard Leakey, one of the world's foremost paleoanthropologists, PBS documentary, 1990).

IN-DEPTH COMMENT:

"A major problem in proving the theory (of evolution) has been the fossil record; the imprints of vanished species preserved in the Earth's geological formations. This record has never revealed traces of Darwin's hypothetical intermediate variants. Instead, species appear and disappear abruptly, and this anomaly has fueled the creationist argument that each species was created by God as described in the Bible."

—Mark Czarnecki, "The Revival of the Creationist Crusade," MacLean's, 19 January 1981, p. 56.

QUESTION 85

Who said it? "To date, there has been nothing found to truthfully purport as a transitional species to man, including Lucy... If further pressed, I would have to state that there is more evidence to suggest an abrupt arrival of man rather than a gradual process of evolving." (A.) Chuck Missler. (B.) Richard Leakey. (C.) Charles Darwin.

ANSWER: (B.) Richard Leakey (PBS documentary, 1990).

IN-DEPTH COMMENTS:

"Instead of finding the gradual unfolding of life, what geologists of Darwin's time, and geologists of the present day actually find is a highly uneven or jerky record; that is, species appear in the sequence very suddenly, show little or no change during their existence in the record, then abruptly go out of the record. And it is not always clear, in fact it's rarely clear, that the descendants were actually better adapted than their predecessors. In other words, biological improvement is hard to find."

—David M. Raup, "Conflicts Between Darwin and Paleontology," *Field Museum of Natural History Bulletin*, Vol. 50, January 1979, p. 23.

"There are all sorts of gaps: absence of gradationally intermediate 'transitional' forms between species, but also between larger groups— between, say, families of carnivores, or the orders of mammals. In fact, the higher up the Linnaean hierarchy you look, the fewer transitional forms there seem to be."

—Niles Eldredge, *The Monkey Business: A Scientist Looks at Creationism* (New York: Washington Square Press, 1982), p. 65.

"Transitions between major groups of organisms ... are difficult to establish in the fossil record."

—K. Padian, "The Origin of Turtles: One Fewer Problem for Creationists," *National Center for Science Education Reports*, Vol. 11, No. 2, Summer 1991, p. 18.

QUESTION 86

Who said it? "We are now about 120 years after Darwin and the knowledge of the fossil record has been greatly expanded. We now have a quarter of a million fossil species but the situation hasn't changed much. The record of evolution is still surprisingly jerky and, ironically, we have even fewer examples of evolutionary transitions than we had in Darwin's time." (A.) David Raup. (B.) Richard Leakey. (C.) Dr. T. S. Kemp.

ANSWER: (A.) David M. Raup, Curator of Geology at Chicago's Field Museum of Natural History ("Conflicts Between Darwin and Paleontology," *Field Museum of Natural History Bulletin*, Vol. 50, January 1979, p. 25).

IN-DEPTH COMMENTS:

"One must acknowledge that there are many, many gaps in the fossil record…There is no reason to think that all or most of these gaps will be bridged."
—Michael Ruse, "Is There a Limit to Our Knowledge of Evolution," *BioScience*, Vol. 34, No. 2, February 1984, p. 101.

"The record jumps, and all the evidence shows that the record is real: the gaps we see reflect real events in life's history—not the artifact of a poor fossil record."
—N. Eldredge and I. Tattersall, *The Myths of Human Evolution* (New York: Columbia University Press, 1982), p. 59.

"To explain discontinuities, Simpson relied, in part, upon the classical argument of an imperfect fossil record, but concluded that such an outstanding regularity could not be entirely artificial."

—Stephen J. Gould, "The Hardening of the Modern Synthesis," in M. Grene, ed., *Dimensions of Darwinism* (Cambridge: Cambridge University Press, 1983), p. 81.

QUESTION 87

Almost all the major body plans for animals appeared suddenly during the Cambrian period, in what's known as the "Cambrian explosion." Which scientific magazine asked the question about why no "animal body plans" have evolved since then? (**A.**) *Cosmopolitan.* (**B.**) *Time.* (**C.**) *Scientific American.*

ANSWER: (**C.**) *Scientific American.* In "The Big Bang of Animal Evolution," Jeffrey S. Levinton writes: "Evolutionary biology's deepest paradox concerns this strange discontinuity. Why haven't new animal body plans continued to crawl out of the evolutionary cauldron during the past hundreds of millions of years? Why are the ancient body plans so stable?" (*Scientific American*, Vol. 267, November 1992, p. 84).

IN-DEPTH COMMENT:

"With few exceptions, radically new kinds of organisms appear for the first time in the fossil record already fully evolved, with most of their characteristic features present ... It is not at all what might have been expected."

—T. S. Kemp (Curator of the zoological collections at Oxford University Museum of Natural History, and expert on Cambrian fossils), *Fossils and Evolution* (New York: Oxford University Press, 1999), p. 253.

QUESTION *88*

Which "intellectual guru" and best-selling author said that scientists had been "fudging and finagling" the record for a century to conform to Darwin's notions? (**A.**) Charles Dawson. (**B.**) Doctor Phil. (**C.**) Jeremy Rifkin.

ANSWER: (**C.**) Jeremy Rifkin. In *Algeny* he writes: "What the 'record' shows is nearly a century of fudging and finagling by scientists attempting to force various fossil morsels and fragments to conform to Darwin's notions, all to no avail. Today the millions of fossils stand as a very visible, ever-present reminder of the paltriness of the arguments and the overall shabbiness of the theory that marches under the banner of evolution" ([New York: Viking Press, 1983], p. 125).

IN-DEPTH COMMENT:

"… not being a paleontologist, I don't want to pour too much scorn on paleontologists, but if you were to spend your life picking up bones and finding little fragments of head and little fragments of jaw, there's a very strong desire to exaggerate the importance of those fragments."

—Dr. Greg Kirby in an address given at a meeting of the Biology Teachers Association of South Australia in 1976. Dr. Kirby was the Senior Lecturer in Population Biology at Flinders University and was giving the case for evolution.

QUESTION *89*

Which book of the Bible said that when dealing with disease, we should wash under running water, thousands of years before modern science discovered the life-saving fact? (A.) Job. (B.) Leviticus. (C.) Genesis.

ANSWER: (B.) Leviticus. Leviticus 15:13 says, "When he who has a discharge is cleansed of his discharge, then he shall...wash his clothes, and bathe his body in running water; then he shall be clean."

IN-DEPTH COMMENT:

"Long before the germ theory was established as fact by the work of Louis Pasteur (1822–1895), Ignaz Semmelweis (1818–1865) of Vienna was able to suggest the contagious nature of infections in women who had just given birth. Semmelweis observed that when his resident physicians and students washed their hands with soap and water before each examination of a new mother there was a dramatic decline in the infection rate on the ward. Today, hand washing is a standard antiseptic technique used by all surgeons in preparation for operations."
—MedicineNet, "Hand Washing for Disease Prevention in Surgery" <www.medicinenet.com/script/main/art.asp?articlekey=182>.

QUESTION *90*

Who said it? "I cannot conceive of a genuine scientist without a profound faith [in God]." (A.) Billy Graham. (B.) Louis Pasteur. (C.) Albert Einstein.

ANSWER: (C.) Albert Einstein. Although he often used the term "God" (as in his famous statement, "God does not play dice"), biographies of his life show that he had no personal faith. According to Einstein the only religion he had was "an unbounded admiration for the structure of the world." It's important to remember that although many scientists use the term "God," they do not believe in a Person who created the universe.

—Don Batten, "Physicists' God-talk," *Creation*, Vol. 17, June 1995, p. 15 <www.answersingenesis.org/creation/v17/i3/god_talk.asp>.

IN-DEPTH COMMENT:

"Einstein himself stated quite clearly that he did not believe in a personal God: 'It was, of course, a lie what you read about my religious convictions, a lie which is being systematically repeated. I do not believe in a personal God and I have never denied this but have expressed it clearly.'

"So, the quick answer to the question is that Einstein did not believe in a personal God. It is however, interesting how he arrived at that conclusion. In developing the theory of relativity, Einstein realized that the equations led to the conclusion that the universe had a beginning. He didn't like the idea of a beginning, because he thought one would have to conclude that the universe was created by God. So, he added a cosmological constant to the equation to attempt to get rid of the beginning. He said this was one of the worst mistakes of his life. Of course, the results of Edwin Hubble confirmed that the universe was expanding and had a beginning at some point in the past. So, Einstein became a deist—a believer in an impersonal creator God: 'I believe in Spinoza's God who reveals himself in the orderly harmony of what exists, not in a God who concerns himself with fates and actions of human beings.'

"However, it would also seem that Einstein was not an atheist, since he also complained about being put into that camp: 'In view of such harmony in the cosmos which I, with my limited human mind, am able to recognize, there are yet people who say there is no God. But what really makes me angry is that they quote me for the support of such views.'"

—Rich Deem, "Did Albert Einstein Believe in a Personal God?" <www.godandscience.org/apologetics/einstein.html>.

QUESTION *91*

True or False? The fact that the DNA in chimps and in humans is 96 percent similar proves that they have a common ancestor.

ANSWER: False. The DNA in bananas is 50 percent similar to human DNA, but no one would speculate that we are "half bananas." Although the field of comparative genetics has revealed some interesting facts about the similarities (and differences) of DNA among different species, it says nothing about the origin of our DNA or the historical relationship between species.

—Michael Matthews, "Apes are our brothers: just ask the Post Office," April 7, 2003 <www.answersingenesis.org/docs2003/0407apes.asp>.

IN-DEPTH COMMENT:

"For many years, evolutionary scientists—and science museums and zoos—have hailed the chimpanzee as 'our closest living relative' and have pointed to the similarity in DNA sequences between the two as evidence. In most previous studies, they have announced 98–99% identical DNA. However, these were for gene coding regions (such as the sequence of the cytochrome c protein), which constituted only a very tiny fraction of the roughly 3 billion DNA base pairs that comprise our genetic blueprint. Although the full human genome sequence has been available since 2001, the whole chimpanzee genome has not. Thus, all of the previous work has been based on only a portion of the total DNA.

"Last week, in a special issue of *Nature* devoted to chimpanzees, researchers report the initial sequence of the chimpanzee genome…So what is this great and overwhelming 'proof' of chimp-human common ancestry? Researchers claim that there is little genetic difference between us (only 4%). This is a very strange kind of proof because it is actually *double* the percentage difference that has been claimed for years!…

"Further, the use of percentages obscures the magnitude of the differences. For example, 1.23% of the differences are single base pair substitutions. This doesn't sound like much until you realize that it represents ~35 million mutations! But that is only the beginning, because there are ~40–45 million bases present in humans and missing from chimps, as well as about the same number present in chimps that is absent from man. These extra DNA nucleotides are called 'insertions' or 'deletions' because they are thought to have been added in or lost from the sequence. This puts the total number of DNA differences at about 125 million. However, since the insertions can be more than one nucleotide long, there are about 40 million separate mutation events that would separate the two species.

"To put this number into perspective, a typical page of text might have 4,000 letters and spaces. It would take 10,000 such full pages of text to equal 40 million letters!"

—David A. Dewitt, Ph.D., "Chimp Genome Sequence Very Different from Man," September 5, 2005 <www.answersingenesis.org/docs2005/0905chimp.asp>.

QUESTION 92

True or False? "Archaeopteryx" has been found to be the evolutionary missing link between dinosaurs and birds.

ANSWER: False. The Field Museum in Chicago displayed what was believed to be an Archaeopteryx fossil on October 4–19, 1997. It was hailed as "Archaeopteryx: The Bird That Rocked the World." However, Dr. Alan Feduccia (world authority on birds and evolutionary biologist at the University of North Carolina) said, "Paleontologists have tried to turn Archaeopteryx into an earth-bound, feathered dinosaur. But it's not. It is a bird, a perching bird. And no amount of 'paleobabble' is going to change that" ("*Archaeopteryx:* Early Bird Catches a Can of Worms," *Science*, Vol. 259, 5 February 1993, pp. 764–765).

IN-DEPTH COMMENT:

"In Eichstätt, Germany, in 1984 there was a major meeting of scientists who specialize in bird evolution, the International Archaeopteryx Conference. They disagreed on just about anything that was covered there on this creature, but there was very broad agreement on the belief that *Archaeopteryx* was a true bird. Only a tiny minority thought that it was actually one of the small, lightly built coelurosaurian dinosaurs [small lightly framed dinosaurs] . . . If, of course, it's a true bird, it is not the half-way, half-reptile, half-bird like we've often heard."

—Dr. David Menton, "Bird evolution flies out the window"
<www.answersingenesis.org/creation/v16/i4/birds.asp>.

QUESTION *93*

The theory of evolution depends on the concept that random mutations accumulate to create new body parts and functions. Does the evidence show that this is possible?

ANSWER: No. Noted evolutionist Stephen Jay Gould explains why: "But how do you get from nothing to such an elaborate something if Evolution must proceed through a long sequence of intermediate stages, each favored by natural selection? You can't fly with 2% of a wing . . . How, in other words, can natural selection explain these incipient stages of structures that can only be used (as we now observe them) in much more elaborated forms? . . . One point stands high above the rest: the dilemma of incipient stages. Mivart identified this problem as primary and it remains so today" ("Not Necessarily a Wing," *Natural History*, October 1985, pp. 12–13).

IN-DEPTH COMMENTS:

"The reasons for rejecting Darwin's proposal were many, but first of all that many innovations cannot possibly come into existence through accumulation of many small steps, and even if they can, natural selection cannot accomplish it, because incipient and intermediate stages are not advantageous."

—Embryologist Soren Lovtrup, *Darwinism: The Refutation of a Myth* (Beckingham, Kent: Croom Helm Ltd., 1987), p. 275.

"The evolutionary process faces constraints far more severe than anything impeding human designers. We biologists recognize these constraints, but we don't often rise above our natural chauvinism and make enough noise about them. Every organism must grow from an initially smaller to an ultimately larger size. Nature in effect must transmute a motorcycle into an automobile while providing continuous transportation. The need for growth without loss of function can impose severe geometrical limitations."

—Steven Vogel, *Cats' Paws and Catapults* (London: Penguin, 1998), p. 23.

QUESTION 94

Fill in the blank. When referring to the theory of evolution, professor Robert H. Peters said, "The essence of the argument is that these 'theories' are actually tautologies [empty statements] and, as such, cannot make empirical-

ly testable predictions. They are not _____."
(A.) scientific theories at all. (B.) reliable predictors of
anything. (C.) ecology friendly.

ANSWER: (A.) scientific theories at all (*American
Naturalist,* Vol. 110, 1976, p. 1). There is nothing "scientific" about evolution—it is a chosen *belief* about the
historical origin of life.

IN-DEPTH COMMENT:
"For evolution to be a fact, you
must have two things, minimal-
ly. First, you've got to have life
coming from non-life—abiogenesis. Second, you've got to have a
change in that life from simple
forms to complex forms over time. You must have the
kick-off, and you must have the rest of the game.

"Now, here's my question: How did life come from
non-life? How did the game get started by evolutionary
means? Does anyone know? Guess what? Nobody knows.
Oh, there are some ideas and people have suggested some
possible ways, but nobody has sketched out any way that
really answers the question. There are so many problems
and complications. There are competing models that
have been suggested, but they're just starting places.
They're just ways of saying, 'Let's start here, and we'll see
where it leads.' There are *possibilities,* but no one knows
how it happened, or even how it could have happened in
enough detail to be compelling.

"Now, here's the kicker. If you don't know *how* it happened by naturalistic, evolutionary processes, how do

you know *that* it happened by naturalistic, evolutionary processes? Evolution is claimed to be a fact, but you can't have the fact of evolution unless you have the fact of abiogenesis. Yet nobody knows how such a thing could ever take place. And if life can't *be shown* to have come from non-life, then the game can't even get started.

Evolution is claimed to be a fact, but you can't have the fact of evolution unless you have the fact of abiogenesis.

"Then why do we call evolution a fact when evolution can't even get off the ground, based on the information we have right now? The answer you get is always the same: *Because we're here. It must have happened.* That's called circular reasoning, friends, based on a prior commitment to naturalism that won't be shaken by the facts.

"Which proves that this is not about science, it's about philosophy."
—Gregory Koukl, "Evolution—Philosophy, Not Science" <www.str.org/site/News2?page=NewsArticle&id=5494>.

QUESTION 95

Fill in the blank. "Most modern biologists, having reviewed with satisfaction the downfall of the spontaneous generation hypothesis, yet unwilling to accept the alternative belief in special creation, are left with nothing. I think a scientist has no choice but to approach the origin of life through _____." (A.) a hypothesis of

spontaneous generation. (B.) an act of special creation.
(C.) an evolutionary viewpoint.

ANSWER: (A.) a hypothesis of spontaneous generation
(Dr. G. Wald, "The Origin of Life," *Scientific American*,
August 1954, p. 45). Even though Louis Pasteur (1860s)
scientifically proved that life could *not* spontaneously
generate from non-living matter, today's evolutionists are
willing to believe that it did.

IN-DEPTH COMMENTS:
"This thing [a scale model of our solar system] is but a
puny imitation of a much grander system whose laws you
know, and I am not able to convince you that this mere
toy is without a designer and maker; yet you, as an atheist, profess to believe that the great original from which
the design is taken has come into being without either
designer or maker! Now tell me by what sort of reasoning do you reach such an incongruous conclusion?'"
—Sir Isaac Newton (*The Minnesota Technolog*, October 1957).

"What has closed the doors of the Academy to Mr.
Darwin is that the science of those of his books which
have made his chief title to fame—the *Origin of Species*,
and still more the *Descent of Man*, is not science, but a
mass of assertions and absolutely gratuitous hypotheses,
often evidently fallacious. This kind of publication and
these theories are a bad example, which a body that
respects itself cannot encourage."
—A prominent member of the Academy, on why the Zoological
Section of the French Institute denied Darwin's membership in
1872; quoted in *Life and Letters of Charles Darwin* (London: D.
Appleton and Co., 1911), 2:400, footnote.

QUESTION *96*

Who said it? "I have said for years that speculations about the origin of life lead to no useful purpose as even the simplest living system is far too complex to be understood in terms of the extremely primitive chemistry scientists have used in their attempts to explain the unexplainable. God cannot be explained away by such naive thoughts." (A.) Sir Ernst Chain. (B.) Benjamin Franklin. (C.) Galileo Galilei.

ANSWER: (A.) Sir Ernst Chain (Ronald W. Clark, *The Life of Ernst Chain* [New York: St. Martin's Press, 1985], pp. 147–148).

IN-DEPTH COMMENTS:

"We don't understand how a single star forms, yet we want to understand how 10 billion stars form."
—Carlos Frenk, as quoted by Robert Irion, "Surveys Scour the Cosmic Deep," *Science*, Vol. 303, 19 March 2004, p. 1750.

"[T]he earliest known representative of the major kinds of animals still populating today's seas made a rather abrupt appearance. This rather protracted 'event' shows up graphically in the rock record: all over the world, at roughly the same time, thick sequences of rocks, barren of any easily detected fossils, are overlain by sediments containing a gorgeous array of shelly invertebrates: trilobites, brachiopods, mollusks.

"...this sudden development of rich and varied fossil record where, just before, there was none... Indeed, the sudden appearance of a varied, well-preserved array of fossils... does pose a fascinating intellectual challenge."

—Niles Eldredge (Paleontologist, American Museum of Natural History), *The Monkey Business: A Scientist Looks at Creationism* (New York: Washington Square Press, 1982), p. 44.

QUESTION 97

Which well-known Darwinist had such belief in evolution that he was happy to believe with no evidence? (A.) Richard Dawkins. (B.) Charles Darwin. (C.) Dr. Gary Parker.

ANSWER: (A.) Richard Dawkins. In a speech at Washington University in St. Louis, Dawkins (Professor of Zoology at Oxford University) cited his intellectual commitment to Darwinian evolution as the explanation of human origins: "We don't need evidence. We know it to be true" (*World Magazine*, 22 March 1997, p. 10).

IN-DEPTH COMMENTS:

"Even if all the data point to an intelligent designer, such a hypothesis is excluded from science because it is not naturalistic."

—Dr. Scott C. Todd, Immunologist at Kansas State University, *Nature*, 30 September 1999, p. 423.

"Charles Darwin presented *On the Origin of Species* to a disbelieving world in 1859—three years after Clerk Maxwell [a creationist] had published *On Faraday's Lines of Force.* Maxwell's theory has by a process of absorption become part of quantum field theory, and so a part of the great canonical structure created by mathematical physics. By contrast, the final triumph of Darwinian theory, although vividly imagined by biologists, remains, along with world peace and Esperanto, on the eschatological horizon of contemporary thought."

—David Berlinski, "The Deniable Darwin," *Darwinism, Design, and Public Education* (Mich. State, 2003), p. 157.

QUESTION *98*

Fill in the blank. Evolutionists Paul Ehrlich and L. C. Birch wrote, "Our theory of evolution has become...one which cannot be refuted by any possible observations. Every conceivable observation can be fitted into it. It is thus _____ but not necessarily false. No one can think of ways in which to test it." (A.) indefinable. (B.) open to interpretation. (C.) 'outside empirical science.'

Even if all the data point to an intelligent designer, such a hypothesis is excluded from science because it is not naturalistic.

ANSWER: (C.) 'outside empirical science' ("Evolutionary History and Population Biology," *Nature*, Vol. 214, 22 April 1967, pp. 349–352). Evolutionists admit that the theory is not scientific, but is actually an explanation of origins. This shows that evolution is not a science, but a religious belief about the origin of life.

IN-DEPTH COMMENT:

"[Evolution] must, they feel, explain everything...A theory that explains everything might just as well be discarded since it has no real explanatory value. Of course, the other thing about evolution is that anything can be said because very little can be disproved. Experimental evidence is minimal."

—Bryan Appleyard, "You Asked for It," *New Scientist*, Vol. 166, 22 April 2000, p. 45.

QUESTION *99*

Who said it? "The extreme rarity of transitional forms in the fossil record persists as the trade secret of paleontology. The evolutionary trees that adorn our textbooks have data only at the tips and nodes of their branches; the rest is inference, however reasonable, not the evidence of fossils." (**A.**) Stephen Gould. (**B.**) Steve Hawking. (**C.**) Carl Sagan.

ANSWER: (**A.**) Stephen Gould ("The Episodic Nature of Evolutionary Change" in *The Panda's Thumb* [New York: W. W. Norton & Co., 1980], pp. 179–185). Since there is no evidence in the fossil record that one species changed into another, Gould came up with a theory called Punctuated Equilibrium. In essence, his theory states that a dinosaur must have laid an egg, and when it hatched, out came a bird.

In-depth Comments:

"It has been through the device of presenting such diagrams [evolutionary trees] with the presumed connections drawn in firm solid lines that the general scientific world has been bamboozled into believing that evolution has been proved. Nothing could be further from the truth."

—Sir Fredrick Hoyle and Chandra Wickramasinghe, *Evolution from Space* (London: J. M. Dent & Sons, 1981), p. 87.

"What one actually found was nothing but discontinuities: All species are separated from each other by bridgeless gaps; intermediates between species are not observed . . . The problem was even more serious at the level of the higher categories."

—Ernst Mayr, *The Growth of Biological Thought: Diversity, Evolution, and Inheritance* (The Belknap Press of Harvard University Press, 1982), p. 524.

"The fossil record flatly fails to substantiate this expectation of finely graded change."

—N. Eldredge and I. Tattersall, *The Myths of Human Evolution* (New York: Columbia University Press, 1982), p. 163.

QUESTION *100*

True or False? Charles Darwin's finches demonstrate evolution because the birds have evolved different beaks, which means they are diverging into separate species.

ANSWER: False. No genetic information has been added to produce the beaks' change, which is what Darwinian evolution requires. Darwin's finches instead demonstrate variety within the strict limits of a single species. This variety within species is what allows for different breeds of dogs, for instance. But since the dogs always remain dogs, and finches always remain finches, no matter how many breeding generations, Darwinian evolution is just not taking place (Carl Wieland, "Darwin's Finches," June 1992 <www.answersingenesis.org/creation/v14/i3/finches.asp>.

IN-DEPTH COMMENT:

"The finch beak variation is merely the result of selection of *existing* genetic information, while the general theory of evolution requires *new* information... However, another problem with using these finches is that the variation seems to be cyclic—while a drought resulted in a slight

increase in beak size, the change was reversed when the rains returned. So it looks more like *built-in* adaptability to various climatic conditions than anything to do with the general theory of evolution.

"This episode also discusses the change in beak length of hummingbirds, to adapt to changes in the lengths of flowers where they obtain nectar. But the same points apply—no evidence was produced that any new information is required for these changes, as opposed to selection of already-existing information."

—Jonathan Sarfati, response to PBS-TV series *Evolution*, Episode 1 <www.answersingenesis.org/pbs_nova/0924ep1.asp>.

QUESTION *101*

True or False? The geologic column presents clear evidence of a sequence of different ages.

ANSWER: False. The geologic column does not exist as it is depicted in text books. "The global 'stack' of index fossils exists nowhere on earth."

—John Woodmorappe, "The Geologic Column: Does It Exist?" *Creation Ex Nihilo Technical Journal*, 1999, pp. 77–82.

IN-DEPTH COMMENT:

"The intelligent layman has long suspected circular reasoning in the use of rocks to date fossils and fossils to date rocks. The geologist has never bothered to think of a good reply, feeling the explanations are not worth the trouble as long as the work brings results. This is supposed to be hard-headed pragmatism. It cannot be denied that from a strictly philosophical standpoint, geologists are here arguing in a circle. The succession of organisms has been determined by the study of their remains imbedded in the rocks, and the relative ages of the rocks are determined by the remains of organisms they contain."

—J. E. O'Rourke (Evolutionist researcher), "Pragmatism Versus Materialism in Stratigraphy," *American Journal of Science*, January 1976, p. 47–55.

A VESTIGIAL CHAPTER
Evolution and Morality

*"It is absolutely safe to say that, if you meet
somebody who claims not to believe in evolution,
that person is ignorant, stupid or insane (or
wicked, but I'd rather not consider that)."*[9]
—RICHARD DAWKINS

Time magazine once tried to tackle the mystery of evil in
the human heart, from an evolutionary point of view, of
course. It's easier to talk about morality once you have
eliminated God from the picture, and therefore any
moral accountability. Notice how the writer freely speaks
about "the rules we know," but notes that we don't always
follow them:

> Of course, the fact is, that child will sometimes hit
> and won't feel particularly bad about it either—
> unless he's caught. The same is true for people
> who steal or despots who slaughter. "Moral judg-
> ment is pretty consistent from person to person,"
> says Marc Hauser, professor of psychology at
> Harvard University and author of *Moral Minds*.

---

9. Review of *Blueprints: Solving the Mystery of Evolution*, by Donald C.
Johanson and Maitland A. Edey. *New York Times*, April 9, 1989, Section 7,
p. 34.

"Moral behavior, however, is scattered all over the chart." The rules we know, even the ones we intuitively feel, are by no means the rules we always follow.

Where do those intuitions come from? And why are we so inconsistent about following where they lead us? Scientists can't yet answer those questions, but that hasn't stopped them from looking.[10]

There are a couple of nagging questions: Where do those intuitions come from? And why are we so inconsistent about following where they lead us? We are moral creatures "intuitively." So why would evolution put a conscience within the human mind? If you are quick to say that our morals are shaped by society, where does society get them from? Perhaps you believe that as man evolved he made up rules such as "You shall not steal," "You shall not murder," "You shall not lie," "You shall not commit adultery," etc., for survival reasons. Why then do we not always follow them? Also, such a philosophy leaves the evolutionist with a moral dilemma. If society makes the rules, then there is no moral absolute. For instance, if society says that it is okay to steal, does that become a right thing to do? It must, if society makes the rules. To follow that thinking, then if Hitler passes laws saying it's okay to eliminate Jews, is it therefore right because his society has made it lawful? It must be, if society makes the rules. And if a society passes a law saying that pedophilia is legal, does that become right? Of

10. Jeffrey Kluger, "What Makes Us Moral?" *Time* magazine, November 20, 2007 <www.time.com/time/health/article/0,8599,1686441-4,00.html>.

course. When we say that society shapes the law and whatever society says is right, it leaves us without a moral compass. Despite this dilemma, *Time* goes on to give humanity hope, even though there is a lot of killing ahead of us as we evolve:

> For grossly imperfect creatures like us, morality may be the steepest of all developmental mountains. Our opposable thumbs and big brains gave us the tools to dominate the planet, but wisdom comes more slowly than physical hardware. We surely have a lot of killing and savagery ahead of us before we fully civilize ourselves. The hope—a realistic one, perhaps—is that the struggles still to come are fewer than those left behind.[11]

Despite the facts, believers in evolution hold on for dear life to their faith in Darwinian evolution, because it offers a naturalistic explanation for this world. Take for instance the answer to the following question asked of Dr. Steven Pinker, filmed for PBS's *Evolution: "The Mind's Big Bang"*:

> **Q:** How important, in your estimation, is Darwin's theory of evolution by natural selection to the field of biology?

> **A:** Biologists often say that nothing in biology makes sense except in the light of evolution, and, most importantly, Darwin's theory of natural selection explains the appearance of design in

---

11. Ibid.

living things. You look at living things, and it
looks as if they've been engineered. We've got a
heart that pumps blood. We've got eyes that have
a transparent lens, irises that open and close in
response to the light level, and muscles that move
them in and out. We've got ears that record vibra-
tions of sound, and lubricated joints in our knees
and elbows.

Who put them all together? Until Darwin, it
would have been completely reasonable to say,
"There has to have been a cosmic engineer." For
the same reason that if we see a watch we know
that there has to have been a watchmaker, when
we see an eyeball or a heart or an elbow, there has
to have been something that designed that. Darwin
showed why that is not right, that you can get the
appearance of engineering in the natural world
without invoking a real engineer.

Darwin's theory of natural selection explains
how we find signs of engineering or design in the
living world; why, whenever we look at a plant
or animal, we see fantastically complicated
machinery.[12]

These are the words of (for want of a better word) a
simpleton. Dr. Pinker admits that the incredible design in
creation logically demands that there be a Creator, yet he
then says, "Darwin showed why that is not right, that you
can get the appearance of engineering in the natural
world without invoking a real engineer." That's nothing

---

12. *Evolution: "The Mind's Big Bang"* <www.pbs.org/wgbh/evolution/library/
07/2/l_072_03.html>.

short of crazy-talk. Point to one building on this earth that didn't have a builder; or one painting that didn't have a painter, or anything on this entire earth that has been "made" that didn't have a maker.

THE PRICE OF EVOLUTION

On December 8, 2008, the Omaha Police Department released a three-page suicide note left by Robert A. Hawkins, the 19-year-old who fatally shot eight people at an Omaha shopping mall before turning the gun on himself. In the telling note, it's clear that Hawkins wasn't the "loner" he was first made out to be. He didn't lack friends. He said, "You guys are the best friends anyone could ever ask for." Rather, the note says exactly why he "snapped." It said, "I've just snapped [—] I can't take this meaningless existence anymore..."

If the secular world insists on saying that there is no God and that we are the products of evolutionary chance, they are saying that we are all mud, made for no rhyme or reason. In other words, they have no real idea where we came from, what we are doing here, or where we are going after death. Hawkins and millions of others are the tragic result of that meaningless existence. Of course, there are many who don't think as deeply as Hawkins. They are quite happy to live life with no purpose. But those who deny God, and then think deeply about the issues of life and death, find themselves in hopelessness.

THE GENIUS

Here's one more question for you. Who said of God, "I want to know His thoughts, the rest are details"? It was Albert Einstein. This is a famous quote of the man whose name was synonymous with the word "genius." His life story is fascinating. As a young man he was immoral and boasted that all he wanted to do in life was sin and face any consequences that may arise from his actions. But as he aged he became more philosophical about life, and about the idea of God and His existence. His desire to know the thoughts of God is interesting. However, God speaks in Scripture and tells us, "'For my thoughts are not your thoughts, nor are your ways My ways,' says the LORD. 'For as the heavens are higher than the earth, so are My ways higher than your ways, and My thoughts than your thoughts'" (Isaiah 55:8,9). Wanting to know the thoughts of God would be like an ant wanting to carry a herd of ten thousand fully-grown male elephants on its back.

As Einstein aged he became more philosophical about life, and about the idea of God and His existence.

Consider for a moment about how God thinks. Because He is omniscient (has all knowledge), He never thinks of anything. He never has a "new" thought come to mind. If He did, He wouldn't be all-knowing. All "thought" is simultaneously present within the mind of God. He sees all, knows all, and dwells everywhere. This is a little difficult for our tiny minds to understand. Think about it—we can't even entertain two thoughts at one time. Try it. Count up to ten in your mind and name ten colors at the same time. So, don't be like Albert and try to bite off more than you can chew. Instead of wanting to know God's thoughts, ask Him for

His will, something He has made abundantly clear in the Bible.

LOOK TO THE ANT

Think for a moment about the miracle of life. Consider one tiny part of creation: the ant. He has a mouth, eyes, a sense of smell, a brain, and legs. He sleeps at night to rest his weary brain and awakes in the morning and goes to work. And that's what he does: work. He hardly stops for food and drink. He knows what he's doing. He has an instinctive plan and a purpose. He also has a will to live. If you stomp near him he panics and runs from your foot. He not only thinks, reasons, eats, sleeps, and works, but he has a little heart, blood, a nervous system, and a beautifully made body. There are not only males but female ants, with different and complementary body parts, made for reproductive purposes. There are thousands of different shapes and sizes and types of ants, all working like there is no tomorrow to store up food and to survive.

Then think of all the different types of insects, and animals, all the amazing fish, incredible birds, and human beings—trillions of them, all doing the same thing—all working and searching for food to survive. All these have the miracle of incredibly intricate bodies and amazingly diverse instincts and wills.

That leaves me with another question. If God didn't create creation, who created it? If there was no Creator then we are left with an insane alternative: all we see in creation then happened by chance. And if it happened by chance, where did the material come from to bring it into its present state of order? If there was an explosion

(big bang), we are not only left with the question about
the cause of the explosion, but also questions about what
the material was that exploded in the big bang, and
where that material came from. Science has no answers
—just more questions. The big bang proponent will pre-
dictably ask, "If everything must have a cause, then who
made God?" The answer is simply that God doesn't dwell
in the dimension of time. He is eternal, and eternity has
neither beginning nor end. Only time demands a beginning and an end. That's why God told Moses that His
name was "I AM." He is neither past nor future. He just
"is." He dwells in eternity, and that's where we go the
moment we "pass on."

THE IDENTITY OF EVOLUTION

Hard though it is to believe that all this incredible creation came about through evolution, many are convinced
that evolution is responsible. And if they are right in
their beliefs, then evolution is the Creator. Evolution is
therefore "God." Darwinian believers wouldn't put it in
those words, but that's what they believe. There can be
no argument that whoever or whatever *created* all things
is the Creator (God).

Idolatry (making up your own god) is nothing new
for human beings. We gravitate to it. The nations that
surrounded Israel continually made up their own gods,
and that's why God said in the First of the Ten Commandments, "I am the Lord your God. You shall have no other
gods before me."

The reason the evolutionist makes up his own god
is because his own God-given reason tells him that creation had a Creator, and evolution fits the bill. He loves

A Fairy Tale for Grownups151

evolution with all of his heart, mind, soul, and strength, because it gave him life and all of life's pleasures. Attack his beliefs and he will come back at you with zeal of a religious fanatic.

But he loves his god for one more reason. His idol has no moral dictates. It satisfies his intellectual need for a Creator, but it doesn't tell him how to morally live. Evolution is the modern-day golden calf. It's a "dumb" idol, and as the Bible says, "Those who make them are like them." All the believer needs to do is believe in his heart and confess with his mouth, "I trust in evolution," and that deals with his problem of sin, of guilt, and consequently of any thought of Judgment Day. It's the ultimate delusion.

The fact is, creation tells us that there is a Creator, and He exists whether we believe He does or not. The Bible warns us that He has appointed a day in which He will judge the world in righteousness. Evolution is a non-issue when it comes to this bigger issue. Set it aside for a moment, and ask yourself how you will do on that day. Let's see, by looking for a moment at the Ten Commandments. Please stay with me, because these are probably the most important questions you will ever be asked.

I'm going to put you on the stand. I will be the prosecutor, and you be the defendant. I will cross-examine you under the light of God's Law to see if you are a criminal in His sight. You have nothing to lose by doing this, if you are innocent. All I ask of you is that you tell the truth, the whole truth, and nothing but the truth...so help you God.

Here's the first question. Have you hated anyone? (The Bible equates hatred with committing murder in your heart.) If you have, then you are guilty of murder in God's eyes. Have you made a god to suit yourself? It's easy to do. Just imagine a god in your mind that you feel comfortable with, and then pray regularly to him. I did it for years. I prayed each night to my own conception of God. He was my idle that I snuggled up to each night. The problem was, he didn't exist. He was merely a figment of my imagination—the place of imagery. The God revealed in Scripture is perfect, holy, and righteous, and He warns that He will by no means clear the guilty. He's not so easy to snuggle up to.

Have you always honored your parents implicitly? Have you always valued them, and had an attitude toward them that is pleasing in the sight of God?

Have you ever used God's name in vain? Think about that. God gave you life. He gave you eyes to see the beauty of this creation. He gave you ears to enjoy good music, taste buds to enjoy good food. He lavished His goodness upon you, and then you used His holy name as a cuss word to express disgust. That's a very serious sin—one that is called "blasphemy."

Jesus said, "Whoever looks at a woman to lust for her has already committed adultery with her in his heart." Have you ever lusted for someone who's not your spouse? Then you have committed adultery in God's eyes. Have you ever stolen something (irrespective of its value)? If you have, you are a thief. If you have told just one lie, you are a liar, and cannot enter Heaven (see Revelation 21:8). We often think lightly of lying, calling them fibs or "white lies," yet Scripture tells us that "lying lips are an abomination to the Lord." That means lies are "extremely detestable" to Him. What will happen to you on Judgment

Day? If you are anything like me before I was converted, you will be found guilty, and will end up in Hell, forever.

Don't you love life? Are you going to let death seize on you and eternal justice take you to Hell? Please don't let that happen. I'm sure that you don't want to go to Hell. I don't want you to go to there, and it's not God's will either. He has made provision for you to be forgiven. Do you know what He did? God became a Man in Jesus of Nazareth. The Bible says that God "was manifest in the flesh," and the purpose of the "incarnation" was for Him to suffer and die for the sin of the world. We broke His Law (the Ten Commandments) but because Jesus paid our fine on the cross 2,000 years ago, God can forgive us. He became a morally perfect human being and gave His life as a sacrifice for the sin of the world. That means that God can dismiss your case. He can commute your death sentence. The Bible says, "God demonstrates His own love toward us, in that while we were still sinners, Christ died for us." God proved His great love for you through the cross.

Then Jesus rose from the dead, and defeated the power of the grave. If you repent and trust the Savior, God will forgive your sins and grant you everlasting life. So, confess your sins to God today, and put your faith in Jesus Christ. Do it now. Just apologize to God for your sins. Is that so hard? Are you so proud that you can't do that? Humble yourself and get right with God while you still have air in your lungs. You aren't guaranteed your next breath. That comes only by the grace of God. If you are not sure how to pray, open a Bible to Psalm 51 and make that your prayer. Then read the Bible daily and obey what you read (see John 14:21).

After you have turned from your sins and put your trust in the Savior, take the time to go to www.living-waters.com and click on "Save Yourself Some Pain." There you will find principles that will help you grow in your faith.

Thank you for reading this book. Please pass it on to someone you care about.

Yours sincerely,

Ray Comfort